WEASEL WORDS

PHILIP HOWARD

Weasel Words

HAMISH HAMILTON
LONDON

First published in Great Britain 1978
by Hamish Hamilton Limited
90 Great Russell Street London WC1B 3PT

Copyright © 1978 by Philip Howard

British Library Cataloguing in Publication Data

Howard, Philip, b.1933
    Weasel words.
    1. English language — Usage
    I. Title
    428'.1   PE1460
    ISBN 0-241-10008-9

Printed in Great Britain by
Bristol Typesetting Co. Ltd,
Barton Manor, Bristol

In piam memoriam H.W.F.

CONTENTS

INTRODUCTION

Human beings have always had a tendency to think that their world is going to the dogs. About seven centuries before Christ grumpy old Hesiod, who felt the presence of the gods heavy about him, was writing wistfully of the golden, silver, and brazen ages of his grand-fathers: 'But now indeed we have a race of iron, and men never rest from labour and sorrow by day, nor from perishing by night.' His pessimistic view influenced Virgil, and continues to influence us and to express a common human attitude to the present. Publilius Syrus, the most popular writer of mimes at Rome in the first century B.C., has left us one of his *sententiae* that evidently rang a satis-factorily gloomy bell in human nature then as now: 'The next day is never so good as the day before.' In our own time Frank Norman has written a successful modern equivalent of a mime entitled *Fings Ain't Wot They Used T'Be.*

Change in the language that we learnt as children is more dis-turbing than most other changes in manners, politics, and society. We call it the Queen's English or the King's English, depending upon the sex of the reigning monarch. Why we do so is obscure, but we have been so describing it for a long time. Shakespeare, in *The Merry Wives of Windsor* (1. IV. 6), said by John Dennis to have been written by command of Queen Elizabeth I to show Sir John Falstaff in love, wrote: 'Abusing of God's patience, and the King's English.' *The Oxford English Dictionary* suggests that the expression is derived from such phrases as 'to deface the King's coin', a suggestion that does not take us much further.

But we secretly believe that English belongs to us, as indeed it does, and not to the Queen, not all of whose ancestors spoke English well, except when Shakespeare was writing the lines for them. None of our monarchs from William the Conqueror until Edward III spoke English as their first language; and it did not come naturally even to the latter, as is evidenced by his small talk

A*

when picking up garters and their concomitant women at dances. The first Hanoverians spoke little English, and understood less. Victoria had a distinct German accent, and her prose style and even her spelling, though charming, were Teutonic.

Departures from the vocabulary, rules, and fetishes that we were taught at school shake the foundations of our existence. A sort of Double Dutch Elm Disease seems to be nibbling away at the roots and branches of our language. So we cling to our superstitions (infinitives must never be split; 'different' can be followed only by from and not by to; do not start a sentence with 'but' or end one with a preposition) like straws in a drowning world, and try not to be swamped by the deluge of new words and usage. All the superstitions listed inside the brackets above were stoutly rejected by the Blessed Fowler almost seventy years ago, and yet there are people around who traduce Fowler as a dogmatic pedant. They can never have read him.

Such a reaction of linguistic conservatism in the face of change is natural, but misguided. All languages, even the most hieratic and conservative, have always been in a state of continuous change. And the middle-aged, and those set in their speech, have always grumbled about it. In *The Frogs* Aristophanes echoed contemporary dramatic criticism by satirizing Euripides for the horrid crime of introducing the vernacular of slaves, and even the colloquialism of women, on the tragic stage. At times (for example, in the fifteenth century, with the introduction of printing) the change is more rapid and radical than at others. We live in such a time now. Since the last war the spread of literacy, radio, and television has multiplied many times the number of people all round the world speaking and reading our language. Their native dialects flow into the central ocean of English, swelling and enriching it, and making navigation difficult for ancient mariners who sail by antediluvian charts.

Some thoughtful people are worried that the rapid growth of English will spoil its universality. They fear that English will be parcelled into a number of mutually incomprehensible dialects, so that, for example, someone speaking Nigerian English would be unable to communicate with an Australian, and a young Chicano speaking his patois would be speaking gibberish in Bombay. We might be left with a crude central core of Orwellian Basic English of a few hundred words and a few simple constructions surrounded by a Babel, in which we had confounded the language of all the earth that we might not understand one another's speech. That was what Jehovah did in Genesis. But it would be a ludicrous and tragic way for English to become a world language for our generation that sets so great a store on the mystical activity of 'communicating' feelings, if not thoughts sharply defined in precise words.

Fortunately, these fears are exaggerated. The mass media of communication are far more likely to standardize than diversify the way we use English. The splintering of the central core of English into a thousand dialects is a chimera. Dialects are in fact dying fast. If we must peer apprehensively into the linguistic future, a more realistic monster to be frightened of is the nightmare that in a hundred years the whole world will read the same newspaper, watch the same television programmes, use the same slang, read novels even more atrocious than some of our current best-sellers (if such a concept is conceivable), have the same mid-Atlantic pronunciation, and, in short, speak exactly the same English. Nevertheless, serious people are seriously alarmed that English is dying, or at any rate sickening, degenerating, decaying, and dwindling into private tribal lingos. To analyse the different causes of their alarm cuts the nightmare down to size.

First, some people are irritated and feel threatened by new slang that was not familiar in their youth. It reminds them that they are growing older, and out of joint with the times. This is a misguided and trivial cause for alarm. It is in the nature of slang to lead a short life and a merry one. People pick up new words for the pleasure of novelty or to be in the swim. Most such toys rapidly lose their shine from over-use, and are discarded for newer ones. A few slang words and phrases become respectable and establish themselves as regular soldiers in the Queen's English. The dictionaries now are full of raffish and disreputable words, formerly condemned by our grandfathers and consequently shunned by their lexicographers, which have in their old age become irreproachably sober citizens of the lexicon.

The law of the market-place operates with language as with other commodities. You cannot get rid of last year's women's fashions or last month's fish, even at a stall in Petticoat Lane. There are soon no buyers for the stale and the rotten, and they disappear. Nobody wants to be seen dead in last year's slang. Gresham's Law applies to money, not words. If a coinage is debased, people withdraw the old coins from circulation in order to realize the excess of their value as metal over their value as money. If a new word finds a niche in the language not precisely occupied by any other word, it usually establishes itself. But otherwise the new generation passes on to newer, prettier words, and feels frumpish and absurd in the slang of its parents.

'Right on' and 'no way', those fashionable shibboleths to the youth cult of the Sixties, which so annoyed those who failed to give the password, are already beginning to sound middle-aged and out-of-date, as passé as old men with long dyed hair trying to rave it up in a disco. 'Right on' was a phrase of soul language from the Protestspeak of Black American English, meaning something like 'you're on the right track', 'continue your present course', or simply 'OK'; cf. the British English of bomber crews in the Second World War 'bang on'.

An eminent Sinologist has suggested that 'no way' (it is impossible, can't be done, elliptical for 'there's no way to get out of it or avoid it', 'Hell, no') is derived from the Mandarin *Mei Fa Tz*, 'there is no method'. An even more ingenious derivation connects the expression with the Vietnamese War in the Sixties and early Seventies. There is a universal Francophone Vietnamese expression *pas moyen*, used in circumstances of incapacity or unwillingness to execute the requests or instructions of Caucasians. It is suggested that this is the provenance of 'no way', with the United States Forces acting as carriers. Whether or not this enchanting etymology is true, the phrase seems likely to illustrate the ephemerality of slang.

But not all slang dies young. Some catches on and becomes 'correct' English. 'Appendicitis' was left out of the *OED*, because the Regius Professor of Medicine at Oxford vehemently advised James Murray that it was crack-jaw medical jargon that would not last. The word was universally adopted eleven years later, when Edward VII's coronation had to be postponed because of the removal of his appendix.

Some slang, for example tilly-valley (a sixteenth century exclamation of impatience: nonsense! fiddlesticks!), is preserved as in amber in historical dictionaries and the Mummerset of period theatricals and the Gadzookery of historical novels. Some leads a healthy regional existence for many years without being accepted into the central body of English: for example, the jolly 'limer' of West-Indian English. A limer is somebody who hangs about the streets doing nothing. From him is derived as a back-formation the lazy verb, to lime. This slang is said to have been in use since the 1940s, but written evidence for this is lacking. It is a common-or-garden word in West-Indian English, and as such is rightly recorded in the *OED Supplement*, although it means nothing to other branches of the English-speaking family.

Other new slang words such as 'happenstantial' (an unduly elaborate way of saying by chance) and 'the flickering blue parent' (the latest *Newsweek* Newspeak for a television set) are amusing or tasteless (depending on one's sense of humour and taste) when they are first used, but soon become anachronistic and a laughing-stock, and die of embarrassment.

Other slang is older than we suppose. 'Mugging', an urban hazard of the Seventies, was defined as 'to beat up' as long ago as 1846 in *The Swell's Night Guide*: 'I knows that 'ere whitehouse warment would chaff—and you knows I'm soon shirty, and then we should have a mugging match.' 'One handsome minibus' was advertised for sale in the *Scotsman* in 1845. 'Pig', the radical chic term of abuse for a policeman in the Sixties, is defined in dictionaries of under-world argot of the early nineteenth century as slang for police-man.

People have been saying bye-bye, as a colloquial variant of good-bye, since the seventeenth century; ta-ta since 1837 (it is said to the eponym of *Phineas Finn*, published in 1869, by an aristocratic young secretary). 'Hot', in the modern sense of stolen, easily identi-fiable, and accordingly difficult to dispose of, is recorded in the *OED Supplement* as first being used in 1925. In fact it occurred in *The Eustace Diamonds*, also by the prolific Trollope, fifty years before that: 'Nothing too hot or too heavy for Messrs Harter and Benjamin' (a firm of shady jewellers).

If new slang serves a useful purpose or fills a gap in the language, it survives; if not, it quickly fades away to be replaced by other prettier and equally short-lived weeds. At any time it is a matter of judgment whether a word is slang, colloquial, obsolete, or estab-lished. George Eliot wrote mischievously in *Middlemarch*: 'Correct English is the slang of prigs who write history and essays. And the strongest slang of all is the slang of poets.' Perhaps there is more slang around today, because more people of different cultures and casts of thought are using the language. But there is no reason to be alarmed by this. Slang is a source of vitality, not decadence, in a language. And generally, by the innumerable daily siftings and weedings of language, it is the useful and pretty slang that survives, the useless and ugly that dies.

A second more important modern cause of change in English is

13

the recent vast proliferation of science and other knowledge, and their jargons full of technical terms. When the world was younger, and seemed smaller and simpler, Aristotle could contrive to make the whole world of knowledge, from Natural History and theatrical criticism to Metaphysics, his oyster. Leonardo da Vinci, that exemplary Renaissance man, could manage to be painter, sculptor, engineer, poet, and inventor of genius, a polymath so various that he seemed to be not one but all mankind's epitome. Benjamin Jowett thought he knew everything worth knowing, and heroically imagined he had an obligation to use his knowledge for the benefit of those less fortunate, who did not always appreciate it. As *The Masque of Balliol*, composed by members of Balliol College in the late 1870s, summed him up:

'First come I; my name is Jowett.
There's no knowledge but I know it.
I am Master of this college:
What I don't know isn't knowledge.'

Though knowing next to nothing of English philology, Jowett even presumed to rewrite the introduction to *The Oxford English Dictionary* and change its title, without consulting its editor, James Murray, the greatest lexicographer then living.

The days of such megalomaniac and piratical attempts to buccaneer in all the seven seas of general knowledge are past. Science has become more diffuse, more complicated, and more specialized. Academic disciplines have been subdivided and regimented into narrow specializations with private technical vocabularies so hermetic that a Chomskyan psycholinguist, let us say, and a nuclear physicist working in quantum mechanics speak languages as mutually incomprehensible as Telugu and Cree. No longer can we merely not follow all the complex arguments of the pioneers of modern thought. We cannot even understand what they are saying.

As might have been expected, this proliferation of new English has been greatest in the new social 'sciences', which have yet to establish their technical vocabularies and academic reputations. In their youth the physical sciences also had the same trouble in using old words like 'energy' and 'force' with new meanings, often for many years before their terminologies settled down.

Terence Miller, Director of the Polytechnic of North London, suggests that in scientific terms sociology is still at the inchoate stage of alchemy, with a long way to go before it becomes chemistry. Accordingly, he does not consider it a suitable subject to teach to

14

undergraduates. A completely new hard-nosed science such as cybernetics (a name derived from the Greek word for a helmsman, and defined in 1947 by its nomenclators, Norbert Wiener and Arturo Rosenbleuth, as the science of control and communication in the animal and the machine) has spawned a prodigious vocabulary, much of it in the sinisterly jocular acronyms of Computerese. In addition to hardware, which is the computer, and software, which is the program (Computerese insists on the American spelling), computer scientists have lately begun to talk about wetware, by which they mean the human brain.

The remarkable growth of technical jargon was exemplified by a dictionary of the social sciences published in 1977. Without even venturing into the verbal jungles of economics and linguistics, the dictionary lists more than 7,500 bits of new jargon from the other social sciences, with short definitions that often make obscurity more opaque: item, a nonprogrammed decision is apparently a nonrepetitive decision not governed by a procedure. It is dedicated to all those who remain unconvinced by the arguments for caution in applying the scientific method to the social sciences.

Scientific method is indeed greatly to be desired in many studies and interests of life. But its application to the social sciences, which deal with the glorious unpredictabilities of human nature and free will, must, fortunately, be less rigorous than in hard-nosed sciences such as biochemistry. The preface of the new dictionary gives one of the games away by asserting that it forms part of the armamentarium of the student. Now armamentarium is an impressive way of saying armoury. Thence it means the equipment of a medical man. Both are more concrete things than some of the concepts of the social scientists. But armamentarium sounds a fine and scientific word.

The new sciences are prolific at pupping litters of new words, and soon replacing them with others. This makes understanding difficult for those of us outside the jargon. For Robert Burchfield, editor of the new *Supplement to the OED*, such short-lived jargon creates a real difficulty. This is the problem of short-term historical lexicography. The historical lexicographer has to make judgments about ephemerality and endurance in swiftly moving subjects. The vocabularies of aircraft, motor vehicles, plastics, pesticides, and so on, change rapidly. Many short-lived expressions that have been used in these jargons fade away so fast that they do not deserve to be recorded even in a work of the dimensions of the *OED*.

15

In 1975 Burchfield put in hand an ambitious reading programme of sources of oil vocabulary, both American and English. He read the house journals of the oil companies and visited drilling-rigs to discuss the techniques and jargon with the tool-pusher and others on the spot. His instructive exploration of oil jargon shows that 'well' was first used in 1799 (slightly later than the first recorded example of 'wishing well') in the sense of a shaft sunk to obtain oil, brine, gas, and so on. From that original well have flowed test well, dry well, appraisal well, step-out well, wildcat well, and dozens of other recent combinations.

Since 1974 the latest technical books have started to use 'hole' by itself and in all the combinations as a substitute for well. Only time will tell whether hole is in the process of ousting well as the main generic term for the shaft through which oil travels to the surface. If such ephemeral jargon causes a problem for professional lexicographers, it is not surprising that it confuses the rest of us.

In due course the jargons of these new sciences will grow up and settle down. Their prolixities will be docked, their superfluities removed, and their mumbo-jumbo made plain. Jargons are the private languages of those who need to say something new that cannot be said in the existing language. They are not strictly the concern of us outsiders. We can safely leave them to the good sense of their particular Jargonauts, who know their linguistic needs better than we can; and even more safely to the law of the linguistic market, which will eventually kill otiose words and phrases.

The sensible attitude for those of us outside a jargon is one of friendly wariness: ready to welcome what is new and useful into our common language; but equally ready to shout 'But he hasn't got any clothes on', like the child in Hans Andersen's *The Emperor's New Clothes*, at such unneeded gobbledygook as ongoing situation (from sociology). The jargons of businessmen, of space travellers, of diplomats, serve a useful purpose, however reluctant we may be, outside the particular fancies, to think merchandizing-wise, to commit ourselves to ongoing countdown situations, or to make *démarches*.

A third and more maleficent cause of the recent rapid change in English is the language of persuasion. Such noisy persuaders as politicians have always used rhetorical value words to herd people in the direction they want them to go. By its etymology a demagogue means a man who leads the people. The disaster, ruin, and death into which demagogues have led their peoples with monotonous and Gadarene regularity from the Peloponnesian War onwards, by appealing to their greed, fear, and hatred, have given their sort of leadership a bad name.

Television and the other modern techniques of mass propaganda have equipped politicians with megaphones that reverberate around the world. And the new silent and strident persuaders of advertising, public relations, press relations, speech-writing, and comment (sometimes camouflaged as news) in press and television are in big business to get us to do or think something that suits their purposes. They may not yet have succeeded in brainwashing many of us to believe that black is white or slavery freedom. But to judge from the television commercials (which are not a disinterested judgment seat), surprising numbers of our fellow citizens can be conned into the error that marge is indistinguishable from butter, or that one brand of detergent washes whiter (taken for the purposes of the trick to mean cleaner) than another brand of the same stuff in a different packet.

The Sunday colour magazines with their glossy advertisements of luxury and status symbols are thought by some to spread envy, greed, malice, and all uncharitableness, as well as fear of appearing to be less well-off, less important, or less smart than our neighbours and friends. The snobbish catch phrase, keeping up with the Joneses, was officially given a place of honour in the language in May 1960, when Anthony Armstrong-Jones married Princess Margaret.

Certain value words of persuasion such as freedom, justice, fair, caring, and so on, are political battlegrounds. Everybody uses them to mean whatever they want them to mean. The United States, the United Kingdom, and the other 'Western' democracies regard themselves as the homelands of democracy. We find it semantically absurd and politically offensive that a regime such as that in East Germany, which allows its people so little freedom to decide for themselves that it has built a wall around itself to stop them running away, should formally describe itself as democratic: *Deutsche Demokratische Republik.*

In the liberal Western tradition democracy stands for the open election of representatives, freedom of speech, and above all the ability to replace our rulers with another party of rascals when we can stand the first lot no longer. In the Peoples' Democracies of Eastern Europe and their totalitarian imitators in other parts of the

17

world, democracy is taken to mean popular power in the popular interest as decided by the single, exclusive, and by definition infallible ruling party: the dictatorship of the proletariat as represented by its masters. In the West jackasses elect jackals for a limited period. In the East the sheep have no means of getting rid of their wolves.

These two antithetic conceptions of democracy, in their extreme forms, now confront each other as rivals and enemies. We in the liberal West cannot understand how a state without free choice in elections, free speech, and a free press can call itself a democracy without standing words on their heads. Those who practise the socialist version of democracy argue that in a bourgeois democracy we are not really free or democratic, but bound in chains of economic necessity and capitalism that we cannot see. This is how a value word like democracy has come to mean black and white, bond and free to different people.

Free itself is another fine specimen of a slippery value word. In nice constitutional theory almost any citizen (except the Queen) is free to become Prime Minister of the United Kingdom and Northern Ireland. Almost any citizen of the United States is free to aspire to the White House. Any citizen of a People's Democracy, provided he belongs to the proper, indeed the only, party, can dream of becoming President of the Presidium of the Supreme Soviet, or, more effectually, a member of the Political Bureau of the Central Committee. In the harsh world outside dreams, however, he or she will not be free to climb to the top unless he or she happens to have been born with considerable intelligence, determination, ruthlessness, and the right connexions. A bit of money to start with often helps also. So does being male rather than female.

Progressive is another good example of a political value word, whose definition has been so eroded that it can mean all things to all politicians. It now means little more than good or 'you are going to like this one'; and it is applied indiscriminately to any policy whatsoever. Literally, progressive would be always good only if you believed that everything proposed by all our politicians every day, in every way, was becoming better and better. Not even Emile Coué at his most auto-suggestively optimistic believed anything so foolish and full of contradiction. If you live under a government that has recently introduced legislation compelling midwives to destroy all male children, or making the work force produce bricks without straw, a good policy will be a regressive, reactionary one:

18

that is, one that restores the *status quo ante* by repealing the cruel laws. Only an optimist believes that the human race is steadily marching progressively towards a brighter future. But only a political enthusiast or an idiot, often the same person wearing a different hat, believes that laws can do much to improve the human condition. Most schemes of political improvement are very laughable things.

In spite of the pretty weeds of slang, jargon, and doubletalk that have always flourished in its hedgerows and headlands, the English language is a sturdy plant. It has grown alongside and survived them all for more than a millennium. Ordinary people, however unlettered, are healthily sceptical of the promises of politicians, and the persuasion of advertisers to spend money on goods they do not want. Advertising jingles become common catch phrases and jokes largely because people disbelieve them. They know perfectly well that margarine (named from the Greek word for pearl, with reference to the pearly lustre of the crystals of the glyceride of Chevreul's margaric acid) is different and tastes different from butter, and that *Scurf* not only does not wash whiter than *Dandruff*, but is probably the same detergent under a different name.

There is most to fear from political doubletalk, as in Orwell's nightmare of a totalitarian future, *1984*, in which the official language, 'Newspeak', progressively narrows the range of ideas and independent thought. A century that has seen great nations led down the road to ruin by lying propaganda, like sheep to the shambles, cannot afford to be complacent about the power of dishonest language. Free speech and a free press are the palladium of our liberty, which is why tyrants hate them like poison, and cannot succeed without destroying them.

But the language is tougher than its users. No dictator has yet come to power solely by manipulating words. He usually needs guns, and thugs, and bribes, as well as lies. Once he has seized power, then he uses it to suppress free speech and distort the language. So long as we are free to say what we want about anything, English is our strong defence against tyranny.

Political gobbledygook is more likely to cause muddled thinking and inefficiency than tyranny. In 1977 Sir Harold Wilson's Committee to Review the Functioning of Financial Institutions published a volume of evidence. This quoted Mr David Lea, of the Economic Department of the Trades Union Congress, as saying: 'I do not think we can say it is a black or white situation but in the

1980s what we are emphasizing is that we are in a whole new ball game when we hope we will have a growth scenario when we believe that profitability in a secular as well as a cyclical sense will be important.'

The sentence is not untypical of Mr Lea's evidence. Read it forwards, backwards, and sideways, and it is still difficult to attach a clear meaning to it. It is alarming to think that Mr Lea is a key adviser on economic and industrial matters to Len Murray, General Secretary of the Trades Union Congress, at a time when the TUC is expanding its ambitions towards an ever greater role in economic policy.

If it is true that English can survive and flourish, rough-hew it how we will with slang, jargon, and cant, why do we need any rules to tell us how to use it? 'When *I* use a word,' Humpty Dumpty said, in rather a scornful tone, 'it means just what I choose it to mean—neither more nor less.'

'The question is,' said Alice, 'whether you *can* make words mean so many different things.'

'The question is,' said Humpty Dumpty, 'which is to be master—that's all.'

Why cannot we all behave like the Great Egg, and use English exactly as we want to, ignoring the imaginary rules of nit-picking pedants and the prescriptions of purist busybodies? This suggestion is attractive to our age that questions all authority. The trouble with Humpty's English, as Alice found, is that you cannot understand what he is saying until he explains it. His translation of *Jabberwocky*, though ingenious, is clearly nonsense. When he says 'impenetrability', what he claims to mean is that 'we've had enough of that subject, and it would be just as well if you'd mention what you mean to do next, as I suppose you don't mean to stop here all the rest of your life'. There is a nice knock-down meaning for you. But you could have knocked Alice down with a feather before she could have guessed Humpty's meaning without his gloss.

Such semantic piracy is all very well for bullies like Humpty and creative geniuses like James Joyce. There are indeed magical paronomastic spells in *Finnegans Wake*: Suffoclose Shikespower Seudodante Anonymoses; the flushpots of Euston and the hanging garments of Marylebone; unda her brella mid piddle med puddle she ninnygoes nannygoes nancing by; no birdy aviar soar any wing to eagle it. But it takes a strong and determined reader to swallow the book whole, not in small doses, and so give a scenario of it.

20

Those of us who are not creative writers use language for humbler purposes: to convey information, to cajole, to play games, to show off, to fill a silence in the gaping void on a sheet of blank paper or a television screen, to make the best of a bad job, to communicate meanings. The essence of communication is that words should mean roughly the same to the receiver as the sender. Of course, not many words have one simple meaning. Few words signify just one thing, like gorse, which is also a great rarity in that it has an exact synonym, furze, and a near synonym in whin, which is used chiefly in Scotland, Ireland, and the North of England. Even the tiny word 'set' is given 148 distinct meanings in one of the most elegant and masterly entries in the *OED*. Words like truth and freedom are so loaded with value judgments that they mean widely different things to different men.

Different levels of language are suitable for different forms of communication. The man who talks like a leader of *The Times* in a pub will soon find himself drinking on his own. Slang and solecism in formal writing put the reader off, and so foul the channel of communication. Speech is loose, inexact, ungrammatical, relaxed, full of solecism and sloppiness. It is the raw material of communication. Only exceptional wordsmiths such as Dr Johnson and Bernard Levin can talk as they write, and get away with it.

If you are writing under your own name, you can afford to be a maverick with words. If you are good, you may use words instinctively and creatively, as an artist, with no need for rules and regulations. The rest of us will make our writing better understood if we follow the Highway Code roughly established by the best of our predecessors and contemporaries. Those of us who work for corporate word factories, such as *The Times* or a Department of State, cannot afford Humpty's licence. If all we everyday hacks used words and grammar to mean exactly what we chose them to mean, neither more nor less, Babel and Pandemonium would issue from New Printing House Square, and we should lose all but our most patient readers, who buy the paper not to read it but to demonstrate that they are top people who can afford it. If Humpty Dumpty or James Joyce were to write in their individual styles for *The Times*, or for other everyday auld clathes and parritch purposes, few readers would penetrate beyond the idiosyncratic impenetrability of their first sentences. They have not concentration enough or time for such reading on the train to work. Anarchy in language is as disagreeable as anarchy in society.

The Queen's English belongs to all of us. It evolves like a tide in the way that the mass of us decide to use it, majestically regardless of the prescriptions of purists, even of the great wordFowler himself, who was quite as funny as Humpty Dumpty, but not so arrogant. Nobody has any right to tell others how to use English, though teachers are paid to do it to schoolchildren and university and foreign students. If you choose to say 'stone' when you mean 'bread', that is your affair; but do not complain when you break your teeth on your sandwich.

Any ineffectual prescriptions found in this book are directed not priggishly *de haut en bas* at outsiders. They are forged in the heat of a newspaper office, primarily to bring some little order into the daily chaos of this particular everyday user of words. I cannot see that the language has been enriched by Humpty Dumpty's recent decision to say imply when he means infer, and vice versa; legendary when he means famous; disinterested when he means uninterested; King Canute when he means a deluded reactionary; and decimate when he means destroy. Contrariwise, he has decimated, or as he would also say, scotched, the usefulness of the first in each pair of words for the rest of us.

But the language survives and grows, despite the perversities of Humpty and the screams of anguish of Canute (who was a great sea king, and knew all about the tides). Its best servants are its talented and innovative writers, whose coat-tails the rest of us cling to. But, up to our elbows in the greasy sink, down in the kitchens of language, we scullions invent what rude rules we can for practical purposes, to make our job and the life of our readers easier. Humpty Dumpty rules, OK? But we cannot all be Humpties. In his sense of the word, IMPENETRABILITY: we've had enough of the introduction, and it would be just as well if you'd get on with the book proper, as I suppose you don't mean to stop here all the rest of your life.

The man who is rash or arrogant enough to write prescriptively about language renders himself particularly vulnerable to the slings and arrows of outraged critics. For 'tis the sport to have the engineer hoist with his own petard. While working on this book I committed a peculiarly embarrassing blunder by referring in an article to the Raj as if he were a person, who could wear a hat (presumably a solar topee), and were married to the memsahib. Large numbers of rajas and retired servants of the British Raj wrote to point out with indignation, or wit, or gentleness that Raj is a neutral

22

abstract noun meaning government or rule, and cannot wear a hat, not even a solar topee.

One of the blessings in disguise (at times quite effectively disguised) of writing for *The Times* is that one's readers include the sharpest-eyed precisians in the world of letters, who will not let you get away with a misplaced jot or a mislaid tittle. Something more than half the chapters in this book appeared originally as short articles in an occasional series on new words and new meanings in *The Times*. They have been enlarged, improved, corrected, and enlivened in the light of the many letters they provoked. I thank my occasional and regular correspondents, splendid word-lovers all of them, whether temporarily full of righteous indignation, or far more often generous, erudite, and witty.

As a result of the articles I was lucky to fall into correspondence with Neil Fisk, and thence into admiration for him, and thence into friendship with him. He founded his own technical magazine, and edited it for more than twenty years; and has the eagle eyes, the sense of humour, and the fine discrimination in language of a worthy follower of Fowler and Gowers. He read, corrected, and indexed this book, and made many lively and useful suggestions for improving it. Any solecisms and lapses that remain will not have escaped those eagle eyes. They will be there because, with insane foolhardiness, I ignored his advice.

For a reporter to thank his sub-editors is as unusual as for a sheep to thank its shearers. Reporters suppose that subbing is easy: it is merely a matter of crossing out the first and last sentences, checking the spelling and facts, and removing all attempts at jokes. Sub-editors know that reporters are feckless flibbertigibbets, who cannot spell, never bother to read the style book, and are careless with grammar and reckless with facts. Nevertheless, the reporter who writes pedantic semantic pieces rides even more than usual on the broad and patient backs of his subs. I thank Jan Stephens, that magpie of recondite and whimsical information; Jimmy Greenwood, who wears his erudition lightly; Leon Pilpel, my learned and judicious chief sub-editor; and the other sub-editors of *The Times*, whose bench is the nearest thing we have to an *Académie Anglaise*.

For suggestions, amendments, discussion, and laughter about the infinite variety of the English language, I thank particularly: Margaret Allen, Alasdair Aston, Professor Denis Baron, Robert Burchfield, Sir David Croom-Johnson, Professor Peter Fellgett, Alfred Friendly, Roy Fuller, Jamie Hamilton, Louis Heren, Spike

23

Hughes, Lord Kenilworth, Bernard Levin, Edwin Newman, Eric Partridge, Professor Randolph Quirk, Isabel Raphael, William Rees-Mogg, Professor Alan Ross, Christopher Sinclair-Stevenson, Sir Godfrey Style, John Sykes, Laurence Urdang, Professor W. L. Wilcock, and Martin Woodruff.

1/ ABSOLUTELY

Absolute word power corrupts absolutely

When the Fowler brothers were planning their magisterial little book about common blunders and moot points in syntax, the Oxford University Press, their prospective publishers, suggested uncharitably that the public they should have in mind was 'schoolboys, the editor of the *Spectator*, and the people who write in *The Times*'. The Fowlers took this so much to heart that they persisted in calling their book *The New Solecist: for sixth-form boys and journalists*. Under such an arrogant title the book would have invited wary reviews, at any rate in the *Spectator* and *The Times*, and would have had deservedly poor prospects. Other titles suggested and rejected were *Solecisms and Journalism*, *The English of The Times* (unfair), and *The Antibarbarus*. At the last minute somebody whose name has not been recorded at OUP came up with the less offensive title *The King's English*. It has since done well.

One of the happiest inventions of that opinionated and original senior wordFowler, H.W., was his definition of a vogue word: every now and then a word emerges from obscurity, or even from nothingness or a merely potential and not actual existence, into sudden popularity. The usual vogue word is not one whose meaning is easily perspicuous to the average man, who has to work it out as best he can. Henry Fowler observed that his work usually has some effect on it. It does not mean quite what it ought to, but to make up for that it means some things it ought not to, by the time he has done with it.

Absolutely, some might say to that. *Absolutely* has recently emerged from obscurity to become the vogue word for saying yes; while *absolutely not* has become the fashionable way to say no

25

emphatically. The fashion started in the United States. There is an example from Mark Twain in 1892: 'Do you mean to say that if he was all right and proper otherwise you'd be indifferent about the earl part of the business?' '*Absolutely.*' The pronunciation is American, with the stress on the 'u'. But the use with its American stress has become widely popular in British English only recently, and in Britain it has a faintly upper-class ring, in so far as it still means anything to talk about such class distinctions. In U-speech particularly, *absolutely* has become a self-sufficient interjection of total approval, ousting and confining to a less elevated social sphere the previously popular 'I couldn't agree with you more'.

The adverb of *absolute* came into English in the sixteenth century to mean in an absolute position, manner, or degree. The punctilious lexicographers distinguish three meanings: 1) separately or independently; 2) certainly or positively; 3) completely, unreservedly, or perfectly, as in 'Why didst not thou, the head, command me *absolutely* not to go?'

Absolutely as an emphatic affirmative to mean yes, quite so, as old-fashioned dons say, came into use from meanings 2 and 3 in this century. There is a fine specimen in *Ulysses*, that rich mine of contemporary colloquialism: 'Was the narration otherwise unaltered by modifications? *Absolutely.*' For additional emphasis *bally* and similar words are sometimes inserted medially in slang use. There is a spectacular *ab-so-bally-lutely* in late Kipling. *Abso-bloody-lutely* also exemplifies this primitive feeling that you can add body and content to words by stuffing them with padding for emphasis.

Ready adoption of vogue words seems to some people the sign of an alert and with-it mind; to others it stands for the Gadarene instinct, mass thinking from the Ministry of Mind Bending, and lack of individuality. As you could guess, the great H.W.F. inclined to the latter view.

Absolutely is a venial example of a vogue word. Conversation repeatedly requires some conventional noise or gesture of agreement. And vogue words generally are not worth getting excited about. They should be objects of amusement and interest rather than irritation. Their danger is that the evil that men do lives after them. Sometimes the gunk of a vogue word sticks in our small and unoriginal minds for the rest of our lives.

Fortunately we are still all free to use vogue words, or abstain from them. By their trivial nature the little creatures generally have short but merry lives. Something else soon emerges from obscurity to take their place. Right on, as we used to say five years ago. *Absolutely.*

2/ AMENITY

The rubbish talked about amenity

In districts whose local authorities prefer dishonest gobbledygook to plain words, the official name for a corporation rubbish dump has recently become a *civic amenity site*. In streets in British cities the city fathers deposit large metal containers boldly labelled *Amenity Rubbish*. It is not clear whether this legend is intended to refer to the receptacles, or to the contents that they soon acquire and retain. In either case the idiom is a curious one.

After the original version of this essay appeared, a spokesman for the Clean Up London Campaign took the trouble to write to explain what is intended by the words: 'This may sound a rather doubtful piece of English usage, but on the local authority side there is a linguistic problem. On the one hand the public asks, rightly, for larger litter bins to cope with take-away food packaging, non-returnable bottles, and so on. But when bigger bins are provided, it has been known for business premises and even householders to stuff them full with a variety of *gunk* from old carpets to crates. What we need is a word that indicates that the said receptacle is for the use of the bona fide wayfarer in need. *Amenity Rubbish* does not have a Shakespearian ring, and the English should be able to do better.' He invited suggestions.

This explanation, although instructive and helpful, missed the point. The eyebrows raised at *amenity* rubbish are not complaining that the name is inelegant and lacks a Shakespearian ring; but that that is not what *amenity* means. *Gunk* was a good word, however, with its portmanteau holding both junk and gunge. But it was a bold metaphor to apply to carpets, crates, and other dry rubbish. *Gunk* was originally an American proprietary term to indicate a brand of self-emulsifying, colloidal detergent used for degreasing. It is now used generally for any nasty, dirty, sticky liquid. An

28

amenity rubbish bin full of *gunk* would be a pretty kettle of fish.

It is possible to sympathize with local authorities who provide *amenity* bins only to find them filled with alien, non-bona-fide rubbish, without approving of their chosen nomenclature. The language as well as the streets can be polluted by rubbish. They might try *trash*. It is short, if not sweet, truly English since the sixteenth century, and economical of paint.

Amenity comes directly from a Latin root, and means pleasantness, as of situation, climate, manners, or disposition. Concretely it means a pleasing feature, object, or characteristic. It can mean civility.

This harmless, hazy word has been taken up and debauched as a vogue word, frequently in the plural. It was once a pleasant term for pleasant things, especially the grounds and gardens known as pleasaunces. It has recently developed a new life in the vocabulary of salesmanship and special pleading. It is applied, understandably, to the more human and pleasurable aspects of a house (factory, town, and so on) as distinguished from the features of the house (factory, town, or so on) considered by itself, in isolation, without human inhabitants. Today it can also be used concretely, usually in the singular, to mean a particular advantageous or convenient feature of this kind. So people speak of *social amenities*, and we understand roughly what they mean.

When a piece of country is wanted for 'development', or a lake coveted for water supplies, there is a vigorous but not always persuasive assurance that the *amenities* are not threatened. People looking for a house in a quiet place are directed to desirable properties surrounded by *amenity land*, and in some cases the suggestions of beauty, peace, and pleasantness may even be fully justified. 'So home again by water,' wrote Pepys, 'with much pleasure.' He had been visiting the Spring Gardens on the South Bank of the Thames, which he found doubly pleasant because 'a man may spend what he will or nothing at all' amid the music of a nightingale, fiddles, harps, and fine people laughing. Now there were pleasures worthy of the pleasant name *amenity*. It would be a good idea if the word *amenity* were reserved for sights that deserve it, and not given indiscriminately to blocks of flats and offices where it signifies no more than 'all mod cons'. Convenience, however desirable, is not the same as pleasure.

The pleasant word has proved irresistible to those who want to make their activities sound pleasant. *Amenity woodland* is said to be uneconomic, though that should not be taken as sufficient reason for not planting it. *Amenity beds* in National Health Service hospitals are for patients who want a little more privacy and luxury than are available in the public wards and are prepared to pay for them. *Amenity centres* probably mean places with club-rooms, bars, cinemas, fruit machines, playing fields, and other modern delights, and would be more helpfully described by a less woolly word than *amenity*. A year or two ago we should have called them *leisure centres*.

Amenity is a word much favoured by estate agents and other branches of the property business. It is the quality that makes a desirable residence desirable; a favoured locality favourable; enchanting views in all directions enchanting; and advertisements for unsellable slum properties that even the rats have deserted glow with promise. In the jargon of the building industry and local authorities *amenities* are small items in a construction budget most easily dispensed with when money is short.

In 1977 we were given the next best thing to an official definition of the new meaning of *amenity*. The Inland Waterways *Amenity* Advisory Council was giving evidence to the Parliamentary Select Committee on Nationalized Industries. The Council wanted to remove the word *Amenity* from its ponderous title, so that it could represent commercial freight users of the inland waterways as well as people using them for pleasure. Its chairman explained to the Members of Parliament: 'If one looks at *amenity* in its widest sense, presumably it is anything that helps the well-being of the public at large. One could say that anything which helps the public is an *amenity*.' One could say so, but it would not be a very accurate definition, and the word so defined would be so vague as to be useless.

Rubbish dumps help the public. Nevertheless, vague as well as vogue though it is, *amenity* is an incongruous word to apply to a rubbish dump. *Amenity*, in its new coat of garbage, is a misnomer that reeks of Double Think and Newspeak of 1984, which is not long to go now. You will remember that the three slogans of the party in Oceania were: War is Peace; Freedom is Slavery; Ignorance is Strength. The propagandist who thought of those would have been gratified by the latest related slogan: rubbish dumps are *Civic Amenity Points*.

3/ ANALOGUE

*Is a digital computer somebody
who counts on his fingers?*

Originally, in Old French, jargon meant bird song. By the fifteenth century it had come to mean *argot des malfaiteurs*. In English jargon has come to mean talk that is considered (by those not talking it) ugly, or hard to understand, or both. This is divided into three principal classes. Jargon can mean (1) the esoteric sectional vocabulary of a science, trade, or some other closed circle. It can mean (2) hybrid speech made up of different languages. And, loosely, it can mean (3) a style puffed up with abstractitis, love of long words, pleonasm, and circumlocution. Meanings (1) and (3) are often confused.

Meaning (1) is of no concern to those outside the group using the jargon. Journalists talk about Nibs (paragraphs for the News in Brief column) and a Must (because it must go in the paper) as a form of professional shorthand. If the social scientists consider that they cannot express their meaning concisely in plain English without inventing words like embourgeoisement and societal, that is their affair. Diplomats should be allowed to indulge in their *tours d'horizon* and other French locutions, if it suits them. When a speech therapist writes 'Articulation was largely developmentally atypical', we must give him the benefit of the doubt, and assume that he means something more than that his patient was not speaking as well for his age as he ought. This sort of jargon (1) saves time and words by a verbal shorthand that is well known to all who need to know. The experts understand what they mean by their technical terms, and these are of no concern to us profane outsiders.

Meaning (2), a medley of different languages, is otiose, because we already have pidgin to do the job.

But jargon number (3), the borborygm of obfuscation, is a nuisance, because it obscures understanding and may be used to hoodwink us about what is actually being said. Thus a politician who waffles about the pound in your pocket may actually be trying to sugar the nasty pill of devaluation; and gritty shake-outs, when you shake out the jargon, actually mean that more people are going to be unemployed (though, unfortunately, unemployment never seems to rise among politicians). Ongoing situations and meaningful dialogues are two popular pieces of jargon (3) at present. Watch the jargon of the professional politician: he speaks with forked tongue.

The trouble is that jargon (1) rapidly becomes jargon (3), as the bower-birds of language outside the specialist vocabulary pick up the pretty new word to decorate their discourse with. They tend to come from politics, journalism, and the other ostentatious professions. An instructive instance of this process is at present happening to the word *analogue*. This is a technical term of Computerese, the jargon of computer men, who are exceptionally prolific of technical terms, as befits men whose marvellous machines can do everything but think.

An *analogue* (U.S. *analog*) computer is one that operates with numbers representing some physically measurable quantity, such as weight, length, or voltage. The more usual sort of electronic computer is *digital*, which processes its program by a time sequence of 0s and 1s, representing powers of two in a binary code. The great speed of electronic signals enables the *digital* computer to perform thousands of operations in a second. In a broad sense *digital* here means discontinuous, in discrete steps of on and off.

Digital has got itself another general meaning in the world outside Computerese. In displays it means giving information in printed numbers or digits from 0 to 9. This usage appears to date from the first *digital* instruments to show the result directly in numbers, such as voltmeters and nuclear measurers. In this general sense London railway termini have *digital* clocks now, not so conspicuous for meeting-places as the old sort with vast dials. The ordinary desk calculator is a *digital* machine. If the numbers are not broken down into *digits*, but are represented by physical quantities proportional to them, a computer is called *analogue*. A slide-rule is an *analogue* device, in which length is the *analogue* of the logarithm of a number.

Watchmakers have recently adopted the name *digital* to describe

32

their new watches that show the time in digits on their tiny screens. What were they then to call the old-fashioned watch with hands and a cheerful face? This was no difficult problem for some bright advertising copywriter. As if their *digital* had come from Computerese instead of the general sense of displaying digits, the watchmakers now call its stable companion the *analogue* watch.

This is strictly accurate. Time, like temperature, pressure, and many other physical variables cannot be seen. It must be displayed in some analogous form. This could be colour ('in the sere and yellow leaf') but is nearly always movement ('like an ever-rolling stream'). The watch with hands is an *analogue* device in no less than three different ways. Angular displacement of the hands is used as an *analogue* of the passage of time; angular measure of the position of a hand is used as an indication of the time of the day or night; and length within the scale at the circumference (printed or assumed to be there) is used as an alternative *analogue* to angle.

This new name for old watches makes them sound new, virtuous, and scientific. Obviously the epithet *analogue* is correct as a description of watches, but it means no more than 'of the old-fashioned sort'. Do you suppose that the public that reads the pseudo-scientific puff prose in jargon Mark (3) about *analogue* watches in the colour magazines realizes this? Jargon (1) from Computerese is becoming jargon (3), obfuscation. How long will it be before Lucas advertises its *analogue* speedometers, and Philips its *analogue* tape cassettes, as though they were something entirely novel? How long before Parker advertises its *analogue* fountain-pens?

The difficulty of referring to old systems after newer ones have been developed is not confined to watchmakers. Only after the advent of stereophonic sound did we speak of monaural reproduction. Only when colour television was introduced did we speak of monochrome transmissions. The advertising for *analogue* watches is analogous to an enterprising manufacturer advertising his record-player as providing 'glorious monaural single-channel sound', in the hope of persuading people that this is one step ahead of quadraphonic. Happily those who fall for it receive something more elegant, more useful, and a great deal more old-fashioned than the *digital* watch.

4/ BALL-PARK

Take me down to the ball-game

It is an axiom of American publishers that the American reading public will not buy books that make much mention of cricket. Americans are apparently incorrigibly persuaded that cricket is a long, boring, dilettante, complicated, effete game played by chaps in caps on a pronunciatory joke called a sticky wicket. Conversely it is an axiom of British publishers that we British are not in the least interested in baseball. In spite of Babe Ruth, Napoleon Lajoie, Connie Mack, and other subsequent demigods bearing witness to the contrary, we persist in supposing baseball to be the game called rounders that we still play at children's parties and old-fashioned girls' schools. We play it with a soft ball, and put out a runner making for a base, or caught off base, by throwing the ball at her and hitting her with it. The Americans had the idea of putting out the runner by tagging him (touching him with the ball or the hand holding the ball), and it became immediately possible and less painful to use a hard ball: at first, a kind of miniature cricket ball. The game has grown up; but to the British it still looks remarkably like rounders.

Until now the British, holding this patronizing view of rounders, did not much take to baseball metaphors. Even powerhouse spray hitters of language avoided baseball, and stuck to keeping a straight bat, or bowling each other googlies, bumpers, or Chinamen. Suddenly and surprisingly baseball has caught on figuratively in British English. These days you can hardly turn on the television or wireless, those prolific forcing-houses for propagating modish new vocabulary, without hearing some pundit with a very British accent pontificating that when something or other happens, we shall be in a completely new, or a quite different *ball game*. To prudish British ears this sounds mildly improper, as well as pretentious. In Ameri-

34

can English a *ball game* means any game played with a ball, like American football, but principally baseball. The pinch hitters of the radio who pup up these fungo flies are probably not baseball fans. They are using a stylish new phrase without having any particular *ball game* in mind.

Even odder in an odd double play is the very recent arrival in British English of the dreaded *ball-park figure*. Literally in American English a *ball park* is a field in which *ball games*, usually baseball, are played: 'He knocked a home run right out of the *ball park*.' In American English in the late 1950s *ball-park* began to be used figuratively in the dense and restless jargon of those associated with the computer industry. It came from the phrase 'in the *ball-park*' meaning approximately correct. In Computerese *ball-park* has come to mean in the general area; for example, 'I know you cannot be precise, but at least give me a *ball-park figure* of what it will cost'; for another example, 'Under Phase Fifteen of the Government's pay and prices policy, a 10 per cent increase would be a good *ball-park figure*.'

The derivation is, as the terse lexicographers put it, uncert., unkn., and unexpl. But I guess, in the British English sense of that verb, that it comes from having a shot at a figure that stays within the *ball-park*, and does not fly wildly over the fence. Another possibility is that it comes from estimates of the gate at a baseball stadium. There were 5,000 fans at the Horsecollar Bowl for the twinight double-header last night. There may really have been 4,852, or 5,310, not counting the two dozen small boys who had not paid for admission but were hanging from the fence behind the bleachers and the pylons carrying the floodlights.

The phrase is still informal and colloquial even in American English. It is typical of the semi-professional cant affected by unimaginative speakers on both sides of the Atlantic. Whether it will catch on permanently in Britain may depend on what happens to our apparent new-found interest in baseball.

However, we do not have to be keen on a game, or even to realize that we are talking about one, to use its terminology figuratively. Few of us go in for archery these days, but we are quite happy to say point-blank, when we feel the need: 'Now art thou within point-blanke of our Jurisdiction Regall'; the English people give this a point-blank denial; a point-blank refusal to go into the division lobbies.

It has been conjectured that point-blank represents a French *point blanc,* meaning the white point or spot in the middle of the target. But no such use has been found in French or any other Romance language. The phrase appears to be exclusively of English origin and use; and there is no evidence that in English the 'blank' or white spot was ever called the point blank.

The probability therefore is that blank in this phrase is the noun meaning the white spot on the archery target, and point the verb, referring to the pointing of the arrow at the blank. Point-blank would then be a combination of the same class as break-neck, cut-throat, and stop-gap. It may have started life as an adjective in point-blank shot, distance, reach, or range; that is, the range at which Robin Hood, William Tell, and even lesser bowmen pointed or aimed at the blank or white spot.

Similarly, as far as can be ascertained, few people still regularly play the medieval cheating game called Fast and Loose. This was played with a stick and a belt or string. A gullible spectator would think that he could make the string fast by placing the stick through its intricate folds. He incidentally thought that he could make himself some easy money. However, the slippery operator could detach his string at once, and win the bet. It sounds pretty boring, except of course for the operator. Confidence men on racecourses these days play less athletic games such as the three-card trick or Persian Monarchs. But although Fast and Loose is deservedly obsolete as a sport, we still play it figuratively, meaning shiftiness, inconstancy, slipperiness, and generally ignoring at one moment obligations that we acknowledge at another.

We seem to have wandered absent-mindedly into a completely new *ball game.* Let us return to the *ball park.* Some sturdy American patriots have been indignant with the snide explanation that such a great United States institution as baseball should be the offspring of an obsolescent English children's game called rounders. Albert Goodwill Spalding, who had made his fortune out of sporting goods, set up the Spalding Commission ostensibly to investigate the origins of baseball, but really to prove that it originated in the United States, with no alien influence.

His commissioners consisted exclusively of old baseball players, bench jockeys, a United States Senator, and other such disinterested but inexperienced researchers. They reported in 1908 with gratifying unanimity: baseball, including the essentials of the modern rules, the dimensions of the field, and even the sacred name were invented in 1839 at Cooperstown, New York. The inventor was

Abner Doubleday, later as General Doubleday a hero of the Battle of Gettysburg. The immediate ancestor of his momentous invention was an American children's game called One Old Cat. This report was accepted without argument as history by even the standard reference books.

Unfortunately, and unsportingly for a land where sport is the opium of the masses, the report was patriotic bunkum. There is plenty of good evidence that baseball was a popular English game in the eighteenth century. Mary Lepell, Lady Hervey, in her *Letters* under November 8, 1748, mocks Frederick Prince of Wales for his childish habits: 'The Prince's family is an example of cheerful and innocent amusements . . . they divert themselves at baseball, a play all who have, or have been, schoolboys, are well acquainted with.' In *Northanger Abbey*, started in 1798, sporting Jane Austen remarks of her heroine: 'It was not very wonderful that Catherine, who had by nature nothing heroic about her, should prefer cricket, baseball, riding on horseback, and running round the country at the age of fourteen, to books.'

The Boy's Own Book, published in London in 1828, and so popular that it ran through many editions, was a treatise on boys' sports with the rules. The chapter on rounders, with a gloss that in London they call it Feeder, describes a game that is a dead ringer (from horseshoe pitching) for American baseball. As there portrayed, a decade before Abner Doubleday became the father of baseball, it bears a far closer family resemblance to that game than rugby football does to its acknowledged and legitimate offspring, American intercollegiate football.

There is no getting away from it. *Pace* Abner Doubleday and Albert Goodwill Spalding turning in their graves like pitchers with rubber arms winding up, baseball was originally British. Perhaps it is appropriate that we are at last adopting its lexis with completely new *ball games* and *ball-park figures*.

5/ BASICALLY

On a more fundamental basis

Samuel Johnson: 'The woman had a bottom of good sense.'

The word bottom thus introduced was so ludicrous to Boswell's schoolboy sense of humour that he sniggered, and covered his confusion by recording in his diary that 'most of us' could not forbear tittering.

Dr Johnson: 'Where's the merriment? I say the woman was fundamentally sensible.'

Fundament is an old-fashioned name for the bottom, but it still just lives, as in Ogden Nash's accurate observation: 'What chills the finger not a bit Is so frigid upon the fundament.'

In the past century we have removed the possibility of such fundamental confusion as Boswell's by replacing fundamental with *basic*. In particular, *basically* has become a vogue as a conventional, almost meaningless rhetorical intensifier. You can hear it used a dozen times a day to mean fundamentally, essentially, or merely 'I am not quite sure what I mean, but pay attention, because it must be good stuff from such a source'.

This fashion of saying *basically* is curious. Even *basic* and *basal* themselves are almost newcomers to the language, having been manufactured in the first half of the nineteenth century merely as adjuncts to certain technical uses of the noun *base* in botany, chemistry, and architecture, where fundamental would have been misleading. *Basic* became instantly popular because of its novelty, brevity, and scientific chic. The immortal Fowler judged that the *basic* words should be reserved for their natural contexts, as in: the elytra have a *basal* gibbosity; the *basal* portion of the main petiole; its capital resting on its *basic* plinth; and *basic* salts, phosphates, and oxides. In general and figurative contexts Fowler judged that *basic* was unnecessary and incongruous.

38

Usage, perverse and wayward creature, has little noted nor long remembered Fowler's magisterial judgment. The cuckoo fledgling *basic* has shed its scientific and unEnglish feathers, and become the regular word, ousting fundamental from the nest where it had sat for more than five centuries. This victory of *basic* over fundamental has been helped by various specialized uses. A *basic* industry, such as mining, metallurgy, and making motor cars, is one that plays or is expected to play a major role in the national economy. In the widespread jargon of wage negotiations, that most depressingly prevalent of modern dialects, *basic* is an amount that constitutes a standard minimum in a scale of remuneration without overtime and other extras. A *basic* eight-hour day is that period of time for which a specific wage rate is paid, beyond which a higher rate, generally 'time and a half', is paid. We speak, too, of *basic* allowances of petrol and foreign currency; of *basic* dyes, slag, norms, and steel. In on-line computing *basic* is a term of Computerese for a very simple but verbose programming language much used by beginners, but not by serious programmers.

Basic English is a variety of the English language, comprising a select vocabulary of 850 words, invented in 1929 by C. K. Ogden of Cambridge, and intended for use as an international language. He called it that partly because it was designed as the *basic* minimum for simple communication, and partly for the acronym British American Scientific International Commercial (English). Like other such languages intended to be universal (Volapuk, Esperanto, Essential World English) *Basic English* shows no signs of being universally adopted, but is confined to a few thousand enthusiasts. As Sir Winston Churchill said, 'It would certainly be a grand convenience for us all to be able to move freely about the world and to be able to find everywhere a medium, albeit primitive, of intercourse and understanding.'

In the jargon of philosophy a *basic* statement, proposition, or concept is one that stands on its own, and does not need other propositions to determine its truth or falsehood. It asserts that an object has a particular property or that a particular relation holds between two objects, for example, 'this is red', or 'this is earlier than that'.

Basic has won. It would be pedantic to grumble about its conquest. However, it is still worth saying that *basis* is a pitfall into periphrasis for writers who seek to impress or hoodwink by roundabout language. On a continuing *basis* is a poor way of saying permanently. On a monthly *basis* is a poor way of saying by the month. On a twenty-four-hour *basis* is a poor way of saying round the clock, or at any time of the day or night. 'The objective evidence that exists suggests that the building of large new hospitals on the *basis* of avoidance of duplicated facilities alone would represent suboptimization.' Here the phrase 'on the *basis* of avoidance . . . alone' would be better 'for the sole purpose of avoiding'. But the kindest thing to do to that sentence would be to take it outside and shred it. It is still worth saying that *basically*, that favourite piece of verbal fluff, is *basically* otiose. Nineteen sentences out of twenty in which *basically* appears would be sharpened by its deletion.

6/ BOY FRIEND

Boy friends will be boy friends,
and so will a lot of middle-aged men

The language of sexual love is as volatile as the passion itself. To judge from the recent proliferation of advertisements on the notice-boards of newsagents' shops, either the fashion industry is branching out into improbably unfashionable districts, or a *model* has come to mean something other than a woman employed to display clothes by wearing them; indeed, almost the opposite. *Model*, like company director, has recently become a useful euphemism for those who appear in dubious court cases, and in court cases about which there can be no doubt, no possible doubt whatever. In *The Female Eunuch* Germaine Greer wrote of prostitutes 'working as hostesses in high-class clubs, as *models*, or simply walking the streets'. Hostess is another new recruit to the language of lust. Massage and sauna have both taken on erotic overtones, as bagnio did in the seventeenth century.

When Christine Keeler and Mandy Rice-Davies, the *femmes fatales* of the Profumo Affair, appeared in court, they described themselves as *models*. They also puzzled the judge (who, for once, did not appear to be affecting that boring old judicial pose of unworldly ignorance as in 'And pray, Mr Silkpurse, who or what are the Muppets?') by referring to a series of male visitors as *boy friends*, or even *boy-friends* with a copulative hyphen, or *boyfriends* as one word. The judge, brought up in the Twenties, supposed that the ration was one *boy friend* at a time for a woman, if she was lucky. Over the past twenty years *boy friend* has acquired sexual connotations undreamed of in its youth. It now carries the implication of an illicit relationship, and means, in old-fashioned parlance, a paramour. Paramour itself in medieval romances can mean a sweetheart with no suggestion of sex.

B*   41

Eric Partridge, a shrewd arbiter of these niceties, judges that *boy friend* came over from the United States circa 1920, and was originally used mostly by Londoners to hint discreetly at sex, whether hetero or the other sort. The genteelisms preferred in the South of England were *gentleman friend* and (for *girl friend*) *lady friend*. According to Partridge within a few years *boy friend* had lost its sexual implication, and meant just a good friend. Certitude is not possible in such matters. *Boy friend* has probably always had different sexual connotations for different classes and conditions of people. But all classes were less explicit in their references to sex in the Twenties.

The first appearance of the *boy friend* in the language recorded by the *OED Supplement* was in 1896 as the companion of another man; 'He went on ahead with his boy-friend.' In the *boy friend's* youth a woman rather than a man was his customary possessor. The word evidently had no sexual implication for P. G. Wodehouse in 1929, when he wrote in *Summer Lightning*: '"Who is this Pilbeam?" he demanded. "Pretty much the *Boy Friend*, I take it, what?"' Otherwise we have just discovered the only instance of sexual innuendo in the corpus of the Master so far identified. The word still seemed innocent of explicit sexual connotation when Sandy Wilson wrote *The Boy Friend* in 1953. It still meant what it had meant to flappers dancing the Black Bottom: a woman's favourite male escort or companion of the moment, with no hint of hanky-panky.

Since then, either our morals have changed, or our language has become more honest; perhaps both. *Boy friend* can now also be used to describe the associate of a homosexual, as in (John Braine, *Room at the Top*): 'Pansies only use pubs for picking up *boy friends.*'

Precisely the same change is happening to *girl friend*, but it is not so far advanced, perhaps because of our double standards of sexual morality for men and women. Frederick Furnivall, a progenitor of the *OED*, dedicated a book in 1892 to 'my much-respected and deeply regretted *girl friend*'. Furnivall was an infuriating enthusiast, part clown, part scholar. He shocked Victorian society by marrying a lady's maid, sister of one of his students, and later shocked society even more by leaving her. He was defiant of convention. His language and behaviour were crude and offensive to respectable Victorians. But he did not intend the suggestion that there was a sexual relationship between him and

42

the lady to whom he dedicated his book; and she would have been horrified by such a suggestion. This dedication would be difficult without the innuendo today.

This change does no great harm, except that it makes it impossible to refer to a boy or a girl who is, in fact, just a good friend. Human nature being what it is, almost any word for describing sexless friendship between man and woman rapidly gets sexual overtones. Look what happened to mistress! In any case, the language of love, being always restless and changeable, will soon move on to other ways of describing a bit of *crumpet*.

Crumpet has recently become popular British slang to describe women regarded collectively as a means of sexual gratification; or occasionally a woman, or sexual intercourse. A bit or piece of *crumpet* is a desirable woman, a 'bit of fluff'. This low, male chauvinist use dates from around 1880, and should be firmly distinguished from *crumpet* as a trivial term of endearment, for example, in Wodehouse's *The Inimitable Jeeves*: 'I say, old *crumpet*, did my uncle seem pleased to see you?' But sexual *crumpet* has deeper roots than are dreamed of by its modern users. It can be derived from *buttered bun*, which has been in low use since the seventeenth century to mean a mistress, and specifically a harlot submitting to several, or more, men in quick succession. Grose's *Dictionary of the Vulgar Tongue* (1785) explained: 'One lying with a woman that has just lain with another man is said to have a *buttered bun.*' As well as making the world go round, love is a fertile source of vivid slang.

7/ CHEERS

The toast of the drinking classes

Open a door for a young Englishman these days; lend him a hand; pick up something he has dropped; stop your car to let him filter into the traffic jam in the High Street; or confer some other small favour on him; and the odds are a set of *Funk and Wagnalls* to a cardboard game of Scrabble that he will express his thanks by saying *'Cheers'*. By a remarkable transition from the pub to the sober world at large outside the swing doors *'cheers'* has become the colloquial synonym in British English for 'thanks'. It was originally introduced as a friendly exclamation or exhortation to be cheerful; especially a salutation before drinking; especially before drinking something that somebody else has bought you.

It is quite recent. Eric Partridge says that it arose around 1945, became widely popular five years later, and has remained so. The earliest example that the *OED Supplement* could find was in 1919 from an obscure, but not evidently a drinking context : *'Cheers—*I'm longing to see you and a Kenilworth together—the two nicest things on earth.' This advertisement in *The Sphere* was evidently not for a motor bicycle, since the Lord Kenilworth who made the machines did not receive his title until 1937. T. E. Lawrence wrote in a letter in 1934 : *'Cheers,* and a long life to your pen.' Some time subsequently the word came into general use in the pubs and bars of the kingdom as one of the most popular and useful expressions in those garrulous but repetitive places, along with 'What's yours?', 'I don't mind if I do', and 'Whose round is it then?'.

Even before it was enthusiastically adopted by the drinking classes, *cheers* had an odd history. It comes ultimately from the odd and late Latin word *cara* meaning face, used once in the sixth century by the obscure African poet Corippus (*De Laud. Justini:*

44

'*Caesaris ante caram*'). The word is unknown to Italian, but came by way of Africa and Spain into Middle English as *chere*. *Cheers* did not surface as a shout in modern English until 1720, when Daniel Defoe wrote in *Captain Singleton*: 'We gave them a *cheer* as the seamen call it.' That Defoe found it necessary to explain the meaning indicates that it was a new and unfamiliar word.

From Defoe's cheering seamen the word was generally adopted as a shout of encouragement, welcome, approbation, or congratulation; especially in the plural the loud, combined shouts (Hurrah, or Huzza, as the *OED* cheered charmingly) and other expressions of applause of a company or crowd. *Cheers* have always been a popular form of expression in the House of Commons, since they come more easily than coherent argument and other more complicated forms of discourse. The Oxford lexicographers explained dryly that in Parliament *cheers* of approbation are expressed by the words *Hear! Hear! Counter-cheers* are answering *cheers* from the opposite party as an assertion that the matter is really reason for congratulation to them.

It is strange that this word should have been selected as the popular toast of the second half of the twentieth century. Most such toasts in all languages tend to wish the toasted good health, on the fallacious but inspiriting view that the alcohol that he is about to drink will be good for him: cf. *skol, prosit, zum Wohl, auf dein Wohl, à votre santé, iechid da*, good health, and various formulae with *slan* (health) employed by Gaelic-speakers in Scotland, and those who wish to be mistaken for Highlanders.

There is an instructive monograph to be written one day on the class, regional, and generation differences in such drinking toasts. For example, old-fashioned and upper-class gentlemen who started their serious drinking before the war, tend to say *cheero* or *cheer-oh*, while the slight variation *cheerio* remains irredeemably vulgar. Eric Partridge dates the emergence of the former *circa* 1910, and of the latter 1915. Note the interesting translation of the word that Dorothy Sayers felt necessary to give in *Clouds of Witness*, published in 1926: ' "He seemed particularly *cheerio*," said the Hon. Freddy. The Hon. Freddy, appealed to, said he thought it meant more than just cheerful, more merry and bright, you know.' In *Noblesse Oblige*, the source of the distinction between U and non-U, Nancy Mitford wrote: 'Silence is the only possible U-response to many embarrassing modern situations: the ejaculation of *cheers* before drinking, for example.' Evelyn Waugh's Guy Crouchback lay awake wondering why he could not bring himself to say 'Here's how'.

The great days of such jocular toasts as 'Skin off your nose', 'Mud in your eye', and 'Bottoms up' were the boozy 1920s and 1930s, when cocktails were the thing. There were even odder ones: 'Long legs to the baby' (circa 1925); and 'Fluff in your latchkey' (1937). 'Chin chin', 'Bung ho', and 'Tinkety tonk' are obsolete. 'Chin chin' was Anglo-Chinese for ts'ing-ts'ing, please-please; 'Bung ho' was an upper-class toast, perhaps with a reference to the bung of liquor casks. 'Good luck' is old-fashioned; and so is 'Here's to it', with the indefinite neuter pronoun being replaced by a date, a name, or an event or activity, if a fitting opportunity presents itself. All these toasts have been swallowed by the voracious maw of *cheers*. If Nancy Mitford were to visit a pub today, she would need to remain as silent as Ailsa Craig itself to demonstrate her U-responses in the chorus of *cheers*. The undying 'What cheer?' survives as the Cockney and mock-Cockney *wotcher*.

It is a curious and somewhat sobering commentary on modern society in Britain that we have adopted as our principal word for saying thank you the formerly non-U pub-word for thanking for a drink. It is a manifestation of our growing reluctance to say 'please', 'thank you', or 'sorry', at all, for fear of sounding affected or genteel. In Ireland all such graces are called 'owld coddology'. Taking your hat off when entering a house is considered an intolerable affectation. Nobody *sells* anything any more. 'Please may I have a Guinness?' is 'Gimme a glass of stout', except after hours, when politeness creeps in: 'Would you ever give me a glass of stout?'

Cheers is now also coming to mean 'sorry', used when you bump into somebody, or somebody bumps into you. 'Sorry' and 'I beg your pardon' are evidently felt to be unduly U, stuck-up, and affected. *Cheers* (more usually *cheerio*) is also used to say goodbye, as a warmer, more matey word, with a whiff of the public bar to it. For its part 'sorry' is coming to mean: 'Please say that again; I did not hear you.' Presumably 'I beg your pardon' is felt to be unduly polite, and 'What?' is felt to be unduly abrupt.

8/ CHINESE

Making Chinese child's play for a computer

Chinese is easily the most popular language in the world. Between a quarter and a third of the inhabitants of the planet speak it as their first language, twice as many as speak English. It is a language of great richness, making delicate discriminations that are inexpressible in other tongues that have splintered off our Tower of Babel. One Chinese character means 'unable to distinguish between male and female'. It was first used more than a thousand years ago in a poem about a hare running across a field and unconcerned about the sex of the watching poet. Another character has more than seventy different meanings depending on minute variations of pronunciation and stress. There is a classic exercise consisting of a short story composed of this single character repeated nearly a hundred times.

However, there is no denying that as a tool for mass communication Chinese presents problems. Since the fourteenth century B.C. its alphabet has used about 50,000 characters, of which some 4,000 are in common use today. These are the very Chinese devil to mechanize.

Chinese compositors still have to select their type manually from massive racks. A Chinese typewriter is a cumbersome form of miniature dive-bombing, on which a really proficient typist can achieve only ten characters a minute. To send a Chinese telegram each character has to be translated into a four-digit number from 0000 to 9999, transmitted in Morse code, and reconverted at the other end: a laborious process liable to extravagant error. It is said that it takes twenty years of assiduous application to become expert in the Chinese Telegraphic Code. And it has been assumed until very recently that Chinese characters were not computer-compatible, as we say in Computerese, the jargon of the technology.

This Chinese puzzle has now been cracked by an improbable team of two Cambridge lexicographers using a son's Meccano set, sealing wax, and string. Robert Sloss, formerly an interpreter in the RAF, is director of the Chinese Language Project at Cambridge University. Peter Nancarrow is a physicist by training, a patent agent by profession, and a Chinese lexicographer and polyglot by inclination. Since 1970 they have been working on a modern Chinese-English dictionary that will be the first to record the vast changes in the language since the revolution. Without a computer their labours would have extended to the end of the century. If only they could teach a computer to read and write Chinese . . . They have.

Like many great inventions, once the trick is explained, it seems child's play—correction, dear little infant prodigy's play. Since the Chinese language consists for most practical purposes of fewer than 10,000 characters, each character can be assigned its own square on a metre grid of 100 by 100. They tried this out in the geology department, teaching a computer to read grid references like a crossword: line 38 across, column 78 down. This was crude and laborious, with a trolley being trundled over a large grid; and it depended on the tolerance of the geologists, who wanted to use the machine to draw maps.

Then Robert Sloss bought some Meccano to give his son for Christmas. The boy is still waiting for it. They had the inspiration of transferring a grid of 66 by 66 (giving 4,356 boxes a centimetre square for the common characters of Chinese) onto a revolving drum. As the drum is rotated, successive lines are presented to the operator. A cursor that moves horizontally enables any particular character in any line to be pinpointed to its square.

This in effect reduced all the common characters of Chinese to four-letter words, or grid references. And your computer can understand four-letter words, store them in its memory bank, and regurgitate them as ideographs, though it cannot yet manage the delicate variations of width of brush-strokes painted by hand. But give it time. The Cambridge lexicographers called their invention the Ideo-matic 66, with its apt connotations of ideograms, idiom, and idiot. It looks like a cross between a rotary steam iron and one of those machines on a seaside pier that simulate driving a car. The characters are arranged in a logical progression according to pronunciation, so that anybody who understands Chinese and is dextrous can soon rattle them out at a considerable rate.

It was absurdly simple, but its consequences are profound. They now expect to publish their dictionary next year instead of next century. Cable and Wireless have developed the Ideographic Encoder, as it is now called, and it should soon be available commercially. A Chinese trade mission has shown understandable interest in the invention that could revolutionize everything from their telegraph system to printing in Chinese. The Chinese Language Project is compiling a data bank of technical information, which pours out of China at the rate of twenty-five scientific journals a month. It has developed a system of translation by computer of Chinese into pidgin English, which is good enough to make a technical article intelligible to a scientist in the appropriate field, who can then decide if it is worth the time and money to have it translated properly. But the invention's paramount importance for the future of Chinese is that it will preserve those marvellously flexible characters. The plan to abolish all characters, and replace them by their equivalent sounds in letters of the Roman alphabet will no longer be necessary. Accordingly, in the year 5000 fully literate Chinese will still be able to read directly the original records, the *Analects* of Confucius, and the other literature.

By a simple change of grid the system can be adapted for any language that uses ideograms. Sudan, Hongkong, Japan, Korea, and Singapore are showing interest. Egyptian hieroglyphs, anyone? Man is a speaking animal. Language is one of his defining characteristics, along with making tools, living in cities, and killing for reasons other than food. The death of any language that has splintered from the shards of the Tower of Babel diminishes us all. The preservation and explanation of any language enriches us all, whether we speak it or not. Anything that makes Chinese more accessible to the rest of the world is an invention of the first importance, worth more than ten thousand best sellers and the activities of all politicians.

9/ COMMONALITY

Caught in the act of corruption

In 1977 the Central Policy Review Staff, known familiarly as the 'think tank', published its important and controversial report on British representation overseas. This excited lively reactions by the hard, commercial line it took about activities that make no visible profit, such as the work of the British Council and the BBC, and of British diplomats when they are entertaining or writing political reports. It was a provocative report, good in parts, silly in other parts; and it challenged the holiness of a number of old British sacred cows, which is, presumably, one of the unprofitable activities that a think tank is intended to undertake.

The publicity before the publication of the report made us privileged, in the loose modern sense of the word, to be present at the moment of birth of a new and obfuscatory piece of official jargon. Usually such words slip into the common currency surreptitiously and gradually, without anyone noticing until it is too late. But we caught this one at the very moment when it was about to burst upon a careless world, as usual too busy with lesser matters to pay much attention.

The word was *commonality*. This was the key word in their report, members of the think tank told journalists in briefings before publication. *Commonality* accordingly broke out like a rash in prophetic articles from authoritative sources about the contents of the report. Quite what the worthy sages of the Central Policy Review Staff thought that they meant by the word could be deduced only from the context, since their spokesmen were using it in a sense not known to the lexicographers. Apparently by *commonality* they had in mind the principle that there need be no difference between the desk man in a Whitehall ministry formulating commercial policy, for example, and his counterpart in the Diplomatic Service disseminating that policy abroad.

50

There were two things to say about such a principle. The first, favoured by the Foreign Office, was that it was political nonsense. The second, favoured by all who care for the language, and published in *The Times*, was that it was semantic nonsense. *Commonality* just does not mean what they wanted it to mean. Sir Kenneth Berrill, head of the Central Policy Review Staff, then found a third thing to say about it. He wrote an agreeable letter saying that the accusation of illiteracy among his staff was too serious to let pass without rebuttal. 'The Review of Overseas Representation may not be wholly free from jargon, but it is most certainly not midwife to the misuse of the word *commonality*.' Sir Kenneth pointed out that we should see, when the report was published, that the word *commonality* did not appear in it, either correctly or incorrectly used. He suggested gently that journalists looking for a topical peg to hang a linguistic article on should make sure that the peg is actually protruding from the wall before they write. Journalists have to make the best of such topical pegs and little protuberances as they can find. *Commonality* had been used as the key word of the report in briefings and articles before publication. After publication Sir Kenneth and his staff in the think tank were the target of heavier gunfire than semantic shrapnel. But the word that was not in their report is an interesting one that shows signs of becoming fashionable in its odd new meaning.

What *commonality* means according to those who have used the English language until now is:

1. A community or commonwealth: a free or self-governing society. This meaning has ancient authority. Chaucer wrote of governors of *commonalities*.

2. The common people: a use favoured especially by Scottish writers, as in the three estates: the clergy, the nobility, and the *commonality*.

3. A corporation: 'The humble address of the Mystery and *Commonality* of Barbers and Surgeons.'

4. Possession in common, community. This sense was paramount in Milton's lines about the parsimonious emmet 'join'd in her popular tribes of *commonality*'. This is the nearest sense to that wanted by those doing the briefing for the think tank. If community was what they meant, why could they not use the simpler word?

5. Commonalty: the general or universal body, as in the commonalty of Christians.

6. *Webster's* allows *commonality* to mean possession with another

51

of a certain attribute: commonness, which is quite close to the sense required by the think tank. *Funk and Wagnalls* allows *commonality* to mean only the majority of mankind.

Commonality, in the sense of a self-governing community, is an ancient and universal element of the government of England. Since the Middle Ages the Parochial *Commonalities* or parish councils have been representative bodies able to levy rates and carry out decisions in their local areas.

One meaning of *commonality* was laid down legally and narrowly four centuries ago. In the early seventeenth century small masters and journeymen challenged the electoral domination of the London craft companies by the richer merchants. Election was by *commonality*, which the rank and file took to mean all members. Legal rulings were sought on both sides. The great lawyer Sir Edward Coke advised the weavers that election by *commonality* meant election not by all the members but by 'a certain select number'. The clothworkers' lawyers went further, and declared that the Master and Wardens of the company 'be likewise the *Commonality*'. The rank and file asserted the original meaning of the word, but in vain.

The otiose new use of *commonality* evidently originated in the United States. A recent issue of *The Harvard Business Review* (an organ not renowned as a well of English undefiled; more as a slough of pretentious and obscure jargon) wrote: 'As the individuals begin to feel this *commonality* of purpose, they become highly committed to the organization's success. This leads to good teamwork and positive interaction, rather than to having talented individuals strive only for personal gain.' What the writer meant was 'community of purpose', and so, I dare say, did the spokesmen for the think tank.

In another interesting new use *commonality* has been used for at least the last decade as a piece of acceptable (that is, specific and useful) jargon in production engineering. It means the property whereby the component parts of one product or sub-assembly are also to be found as component parts of other products and sub-assemblies. For example, if a new model of engine were to succeed an earlier version in manufacture, but the new model contained very few new components, it would have a high degree of *commonality* with the old model. The concept underlying this use of the word is necessary, because the degree to which different manufactured items have parts in common is important to the organization of manufacturing. Since the alternative is an awkward string

52

of words, this is a case where jargon is acceptable and desirable.

This piece of engineering jargon seems quite close to the sense required by the spokesmen for the think tank. Furthermore, it would seem appropriate if undesirable that modern diplomats should be regarded as component parts of a machine. That report of the Central Policy Review Staff had provocative, and may have had some important, things to say about Britain's foreign services. But its advance spokesmen crying in the wilderness of Whitehall made it difficult for anybody who cared for the language to take their findings seriously, by adopting so sloppy, trendy, and erroneous a word as *commonality* as the key concept of their report.

10/ CONFRONTATION

Two-faced on a collision course

Over the past decade and a half *confrontation* has acquired a new and euphemistic political meaning to describe an old political activity. In extreme cases the vogue word *confrontation* has become a polite way of describing an unprovoked act of aggression. Those doing the confronting are so cocksure of their own self-righteousness that they accuse their opponents, usually 'the Establishment', of 'violence'. This is often an odd new passive and inconspicuous sort of violence, which consists merely of disagreeing with the opinions or politics of the confronters. These extreme confronters seek to disguise their own active and unprovoked violence in sheep's clothing by describing it with the woolly but vaguely commendatory name of *confrontation*. It sounds the heroic sort of posture that tyrannicides adopt towards tyrants.

If our side is doing the confronting, *confrontation* is a heroic activity. If the jack-boot is on the other foot, and the other side is doing the confronting, *confrontation* changes its face and becomes pejorative. There was disagreement in 1977 about who was doing the *confrontation* in the Grunwick dispute, George Ward and those of his workers who had not gone on strike processing films in his factory in North London, or the strikers and thousands of supporting pickets besieging his gates. Some union leaders now seem to use *confrontation* to mean failure to accede to or agree with any trade union demand or request. Len Murray, General Secretary of the Trades Union Congress, said during the Grunwick battle: 'These islands cannot survive on a doctrine of *confrontation*.'

It would be easier to agree with this sentiment if we could establish what the Janus word means. Its modern figurative use is a mystery, because it has become a political value word. You can have an eyeball-to-eyeball *confrontation*, which sounds painful,
54

particularly if one of the confronters is wearing contact lenses. When the eyeballs are out of range, you can have a head-to-head summit, for which the prudent head of state wears a crash helmet. You can also have a direct *confrontation*, which implies that there can be indirect *confrontations* of secondary and tertiary kinds, presumably done with mirrors, or representatives substituting for the head of state and the national eyeballs.

For once we can date the birth of a vogue word quite precisely. The Cuban missile crisis in 1963 in those tense days after October 22 came to be widely seen and described as a dramatic *confrontation* of American and Soviet power. Words played an extremely important part in that *confrontation*. It was a stroke of semantic genius by Jack Kennedy to describe what the United States Navy was doing to Cuba as a quarantine rather than the more bellicose (and more accurate) blockade. From that point *confrontation* passed into common use to mean the coming of countries, parties, factions, or people face to face in a state of political tension, with or without actual conflict. In 1963 again *confrontation* was the specious contranomer and lying vogue word that President Sukarno selected to describe what Indonesia was doing to Malaysia. It sounded impressive. What it actually meant was intimidation, guerrilla warfare, arson, loot, murder, and confiscation.

Until its recent conversion to the seamy side of politics *confrontation* had led a blameless life for three and a half centuries, mainly in lawyers' jargon. It comes from the Latin words for 'together' and 'forehead', and means the bringing of persons face to face, especially for examination and eliciting of the truth. Specifically in the law courts it means the bringing face to face of an accused person and his accusing witness, especially in the legal phrase *right of confrontation*. All the examples of this primary use in the *Oxford English Dictionary* are taken from the law, starting back in the Star Chamber. There is a secondary meaning: the action of bringing face to face, or together, for comparison, as in the *confrontation* of an artist's work and Nature's.

Today, with vastly increased populations, there are so many more faces around that opportunities for old-time *confrontations* have been superseded by the one-way face addressing the people at large on television. It is not surprising that people who are fed up with always being addressed wholesale as a public meeting, when they want genuine face to face *confrontation*, will answer back showing dissatisfied and aggressive faces.

55

The new political use of *confrontation* has spawned the ugly adjective *confrontationist*, meaning seeking, supporting, or advocating *confrontation*. The *confrontationist* politicians of our time have learnt the value of not committing violence, but provoking it. It makes them the good guys when they retaliate. It can only be a matter of time before the popular and profitable activity turns *a confrontationist* into a noun standing on its own. A subsidiary use of *confrontationist* describes clashing with traditional values or methods, which is what *confrontationist* artists do, or think they do.

There is no great harm in this euphemistic new use of *confrontation*, at least for those who recognize that fine words butter no parsnips, but have always been used to cover foul deeds. We live in a violent and confusing age. The violence and confusion are not removed by calling them *confrontation*.

11/ CONSULTATION

The party games that politicians play

The *consultative* referendum on devolved government for Scotland and Wales has crowned *consultation* as the most fashionable canting catchword of modern politics, but reduced its meaning to the merest puff of hazy connotation. Almost all politicians who need to be re-elected claim to be in favour of *consultation*, on the same grounds that they claim to be on the side of liberty, democracy, participation, and the common man, particularly if he has a vote. What they mean by *consultation*, however, is by no means either clear or consistent. What they ought to mean is the action of *consulting* or taking counsel together: a process in which various opinions are listened to, and a common decision or opinion, based upon the best advice available, evolves.

The word came into English from French in the sixteenth century. Its ultimate root is the Latin *consultare*, the frequentative verb formed from the past participle stem of *consulere*, to take counsel. Shakespeare made Richard III say on Bosworth Field on the eve of the battle:

> 'Come, gentlemen,
> Let us *consult* upon tomorrow's business.'

His *consultation* did not save Richard from himself falling into the blind cave of eternal night on the morrow.

Since Bosworth *consultation* has acquired a number of specialized meanings. It can mean a conference at which the parties, for example lawyers or doctors, *consult* or deliberate. Modern legal usage confines this sense to meetings with more than one counsel present. You can have a *consultation* with your doctor on your own. But you must be able to afford the fees of at least two lawyers simultaneously before you can properly describe your meeting with them as a *consultation*. The word can mean the action of *consult-*

ing, for instance, a book. 'By the *consultation* of books temptations to petulance are avoided.' And, in an esoteric meaning from historical English law, *consultation* means a writ by which a cause, having been removed by prohibition out of the ecclesiastical court, is returned thither. In this sense its use is slight today.

The vogue political use of *consultation* has little connexion with any of these precise and unambiguous meanings. Sometimes it seems to be used as a catchword to describe a process that is a substitute for thought or action, or an excuse for procrastination. Sometimes it means a process (regrettably, almost always an ongoing one) or, also regrettably, a situation whereby or wherein representatives of local or national government, unshakably convinced of their own correctitude, but uneasily aware of the need for the appearance of full, democratic, public discussion, inform members of the public of decisions that have been taken, are irrevocable, and, in any case, are much too important to be left to the layman.

A charming example of the word's fashionable and useful spissitude was given in Eynsham Primary School's pantomime in 1977. The Evil Queen was speaking to her counsellors:

'Now I am going off to think of a Plan. When I return you can tell me what a good Plan it is: that is what we Rulers call *Consultation*.'

Sometimes, no doubt, politicians mean by the incantation of *consultation* that they actually are prepared to listen to views other than their own and their party line before coming to a decision. But in its fashionable use, the more a politician spouts about *consultation*, the more his audience should resign themselves to accepting a *fait accompli* that nothing that they say or do can change.

While we are considering party games, we might take into consideration the odd habit of Prime Ministers *to reshuffle*: a practice that is semantically amusing rather than dangerous. It has recently become common for politicians and political commentators to describe changes in the Cabinet, or, for that matter, the Shadow Cabinet, as a *reshuffle*. This unintentionally suggests card-sharping. To shuffle is to throw the cards in a pack into disorder, or to rearrange them in a random manner. This, surely, is something that political leaders never do, or, at any rate, never seek to do, or, at all events, never wish to seem to do. Moreover, when in politics a Cabinet pack is rearranged, some cards usually drop out and other cards are introduced. Around the less frivolous tables at Crockford's such an odd system of shuffling would be frowned upon.

58

At cards a *reshuffle* could take place only if, immediately after a shuffle, the cards fell on the floor, one or more of them face upwards. So far as we can tell from the austere and lapidary prose of the Public Records, this has never happened to any Cabinet, however unfortunate or drunk. Even the Crossman *Diaries* mention no such supine collapse.

Another game favoured by commentators to describe Cabinet changes is musical chairs. This suggests that political journalists are more at home in the lobbies than in their Sunday suits at children's parties. The essence of musical chairs (at any rate the simple version) is that the players fall out of the game one by one, until only the winner is left. A Cabinet withering away in this fashion would have the novelty but hardly the superficial attraction of a gimmick. It was not what Dick Crossman had in mind when he argued that Britain was moving from government by Cabinet to government by President.

A political commentator recently suggested that there was a more subtle case for political musical chairs in the Conservative Party than the regular instinct of party leaders to display some new faces: 'Too many of the heavyweights at Mrs Thatcher's disposal are under-employed.' Mrs Thatcher is too prudent a housewife to hazard her home, which she has so recently repainted, by setting her heavyweights to play musical chairs in it. In short, the political commentator who chooses to describe Party Games in terms of party games should be careful how he chooses his game. However, if he were to follow this literal-minded prescription, he would detract from the liveliness of political writing and the gaiety of nations.

12/ CREDIBILITY

*How to believe as many as six impossible
things before breakfast*

After four centuries of blameless and boring life with a precise
denotation, the respectable abstract noun *credibility* has recently
been picked up as a shameless vogue word. It has accordingly
become skittish in its old age, broken out of its narrow semantic
home, and started to trespass in the territories of other words. It is
now widely used to mean credit, credence, the ability to persuade
or impress others, the qualifications to make people believe what
you say, and Heaven knows what else (though Gabriel himself
might be hard pressed to explain exactly what Heaven has in mind).

A descendant of the Latin patriarch *credo*, 'I believe', the word
wears its original meaning like a Roman nose on its Latinate face.
It was introduced into English to mean the quality of being credible,
or an instance of this quality. The judicious Richard Hooker, the
theologian and inventor of the theory of 'original contract' as a
basis of sovereignty in England, attempted a convoluted definition
in 1594: 'Sith the ground of credit is the *credibility* of things
credited; and things are made credible either by the known condition and quality of the utterer, or by the manifest likelihood of
truth which they have in themselves.' Quite so.

Then in the 1960s it was adopted as a technical term in the
horrendous jargon of nuclear deterrence for thinking about the
unthinkable in Herman-Kahn-Speak. It was used in contexts of a
defence policy based on the theory of the effectiveness of a nuclear
deterrent. Strategists started to write such things as that there would
be no gain in the *credibility* of the deterrent if NATO became an
atomic power, and that worry about the *credibility* of massive
retaliation so long as America alone had the power to start it had

60

been racking NATO for several years. From BombSpeak this new sort of *credibility*, meaning that potential enemies believe that you mean business, has escalated, as they say in the jargon, into the common language.

In particular, the Vietnam War and Watergate popularized the concept of a *credibility gap*, which was a new and pernicious euphemism for calling somebody a liar. *Credibility gap* means disbelief: the yawning chasm between public office and what the public believe. Official American statements could no longer be taken on trust. The growing doubt and cynicism concerning pronouncements by Lyndon Johnson's administration were delicately described as a *credibility gap*. It meant that somebody, usually that ubiquitous character Mr A. N. Official Spokesman, was lying. GIs in South Vietnam began to wear buttons proclaiming: 'Ambushed at *credibility gap*.' Mr Spokesman himself, Johnson's Press Secretary, Bill Moyers, remarked wryly: 'The *credibility gap* is getting so bad we can't even believe our own leaks.' Walter Lippmann gave a more sombre definition: 'The *credibility gap* today is not the result of honest misunderstanding between the President and the press in this complicated world. It is the result of a deliberate policy of artificial manipulation of official news.'

Thus *credibility gap* has come to mean a disinclination to believe a person, especially a public person, or a statement, especially an official statement. It means a disparity between the facts and what is said or written about them: 'We do not recognize them, helmeted, in a bomber aiming cans of napalm at a thatched village. We have a *credibility gap*.' In a similarly malodorous obfuscation Richard Nixon's press office used to announce that a statement made previously was *inoperative*, when they meant that it was untrue. So now to say that somebody has a serious *credibility gap* has become the modish and mischievous way of saying that he or she is a liar. When first used it was a witty and devastating meiosis for suggesting that President Johnson might be guilty of terminological inexactitude. The mischief is that to have a *credibility gap* sounds so much more respectable than telling lies, and may persuade people that there is no great harm in having one or telling them.

Credibility has now become so ragingly fashionable a word in business and other jargons that it is used as an impressive noise, with only a faint appendage of meaning. An advertisement asks for accounting *credibility*, meaning, I suppose, that prospective employers, customers, and auditors will be impressed by your knowledge of accountancy. It is said that candidates for jobs will have more *credibility* if they have certain qualifications or experience. This means that such candidates will stand a better chance of getting the job. A political tract speaks of communicator *credibility*, which presumably means either the power of conveying that you have something worth saying, or the power of making people believe what you say.

This meaningless versatility of *credibility* would be incredible, if its profligate career were not a common one for vogue words. On the usual pattern it will soon have been so over-used that it will be leached of all meaning. Even the most insensitive users of English will realize that the word is making them a laughing-stock. The trendy mob can then move on to some new word, and leave *credibility* to retire to its humble but useful work in the lexical *armamentarium*.

13/ DATA

Data is not what they used to be

In spite of protests from the purists that they are a Latin plural, *data* stubbornly persists in trying to become an English singular as *agenda* and *stamina* did before it/them. The *media* have/has a similar proclivity as in 'the mass *media* is responsible' for something or other; usually and regrettably in the way of the world something that vexes the writer, who wants to lump the *media* together, without thinking of them as one *medium*, and another *medium*, and a third, and all the others. It is a notable recent *phenomena* that one *criteria* of education in an influential *strata* of the community is to be good at criticizing what the *media* is saying about all this *data* on the decay of English. Instead of crying barbarism, it is more constructive to investigate why this should be happening. Fewer people know Latin and Greek these days, and accordingly there are fewer around to be pained by outrages upon their methods of word-formation. And, in any case, English grammar evolves with majestic disregard for the susceptibilities of classical scholars.

English belongs to all of us, to change it as we want. We have made more fundamental changes to it in the past than altering the number of a few words from plural to singular. Think of the alarm that thoughtful Anglo-Saxons must have felt when they realized that the progressive simplification of Old English, particularly the loss of grammatical gender, was leading them away from mainland Europe and into an unpredictable grammatical isolation. Yet no whisper of such alarm comes down to us in their chronicles or linguistic laws. Perhaps they were less hypochondriac about their robust language than we are.

The distinction between singular and plural is not as clear-cut as it appears at first thought. It compels users of English to choose between one thing and any number from two to infinity, which are

63

lumped together as plural. The old dual number, the inflected form expressing two or a pair, is the historic binary plural for referring to twos. It flourished in a number of languages, including Classical Greek and Gothic, and survives vestigially in English in 'both', 'either', and 'whether', and the ease with which we can refer to a pair and a couple as compared with a trio and a foursome. Trousers, which customarily have two legs, are plural, though we refer to a pair of them. In French they are singular, *le pantalon.* But a bra, back in the dim days when such things were worn, was inescapably bipartite but invariably singular. Why should bathing-trunks, which have three openings of roughly equal size, be a pair of anything?

Professor Randolph Quirk, the Quain Professor of English Language and Literature at University College, London, is a brilliantly perceptive exegete of the quirks and quiddities of grammar. The Survey of English Usage at University College has since 1959 been fruitfully exploring and recording English grammar as it is spoken and written today. In November 1977 Randolph Quirk advanced a characteristically entertaining and persuasive explanation of why such plurals as *data* persist in changing number and turning singular. He describes *data* as an 'aggregate' noun. And he defines such a noun as one in which the essential thing is choosing to ignore the individual components, and considering the collection as though it were a packaged unit. An aggregate noun is capable of being counted if it has to be, like sheep, but precise enumeration is not its point. We do not usually talk about three *data,* or 423 *data,* or of isolating one *datum* from the *data.* With the explosive increase in the quantities of *data* that modern science feels it necessary to handle, and (through computers) finds it possible to handle, the individual *datum* becomes decreasingly relevant. Small numbers of *data* become as embarrassing to enumerate as wild oats. We find it less obvious to conceive of *data* as consisting of *datum* upon *datum* upon *datum.* Above all, the word is used as a singular since it is merely the aggregates of *data,* considered as an indistinct mass like butter, that influence decision-making.

The same thing happened to *stamina,* another Latin plural. In English the singular *stamen* originally meant the warp of a textile fabric, a thread, and thence the supposed germinal principle or impulse in which the future characteristics of any nascent existence are implicit. *Stamina* became a singular aggregate noun because the individual '*stamens*' or fibres are irrelevant in considering the aggregate notion of vigour of bodily constitution. *Stamina* has gradually turned singular, but it was still plural at the time of Jonathan Swift. Similarly *media* are/is becoming an aggregate singular, because it is convenient in many contexts to think of the organs that influence public opinion as a single brass band, without separating it into its component instruments, as newspapers, magazines, television, and radio. The uneducated and impassioned often speak on television of the *media* and the press, so confining the word to broadcasting and giving it a new twist that spoils its usefulness.

The same thing happened to *news*. In the writings of such confident authorities as Queen Victoria and Benjamin Jowett the *news* are plural, like *les nouvelles* and *die informationen*. There is an agreeable legend at *The Times*, which may even have a basis of truth, though the manner of addressing the editor has evidently been brought up to date. During the Crimean War John Thaddeus Delane, the great editor of *The Times*, cabled William Howard Russell, the first war correspondent: 'Are there any *news*?' Back down the wires the electric message came: 'Not a damned *new*.' Since those brave days we have come to think of *news* as an aggregate singular instead of a plural catalogue of items of *news*.

As we should expect, Professor Quirk's opinion is solidly rooted in the historical *data* of the word. *Data* started to change number in Computerese, the jargon of men who work with such vast quantities of *data* that the notion of enumerating them is as absurd as the notion of a farmer counting his wheat. No doubt it could be done, as scientists have calculated the number of atoms in the Universe, but it is not a calculation that one wants to do often.

The shift to thinking and speaking about *data* as an aggregate singular is recorded as occurring in the technical literature of computers from the 1960s. From there it spread into journalism and other general writing (*Science Journal*, 1970): 'During each orbit *data* from the experiment is transmitted from the satellite to Fairbanks in Alaska, and from there to Oxford for initial processing.' A dictionary of computers in the same year made an interesting distinction: '*Data* is sometimes contrasted with information, which is said to result from the processing of *data*.'

The language and cast of mind of those who work with computers incline them to think of *data* as an aggregate singular. *Data* is put in a bank, like the singular money, handled, and transmitted over a *data link*. *Data* processing is an automatic and continuous process as innumerable as the barley being processed by a combine. A *data logger* records the successive values of a number of different physical quantities.

The computermen have got it into their noddles that *data* is an aggregate singular like English porridge. James Murray, the founding father of the *OED*, was reported by his granddaughter to have complained: 'These porridge aren't properly cooked'; and some professional Scots still refer to their porridge as 'they' or 'them'. There is evidently no future in outsiders protesting that they are wrong to say things like: '*Data* that is four to twelve years old is of limited use.' Those of us whose atavistic Latinate sensibilities are outraged by the practice can avoid copying it, until perhaps usage drags us willy-nilly to conform, as it has with *stamina*. We certainly ought to refrain from adopting such Computerese as *data base* figuratively, when all that we mean is records, and to abstain from saying, or writing, the *media*, when all that we mean is the newspapers, or the telly.

And we can reflect with the tolerant but acute Randolph Quirk that the rise of the aggregate singular nastily illustrates the further relegation of the individual. If we start talking about a *strata* of society as a singular, as the sociologists do, we may forget that inside each homogeneous group large numbers of people, each one an individual, are struggling to get out. Is this the direction of English 1984? Professor Quirk comes to no firm conclusion, but his *data* are/is stimulating.

14/ DICHOTOMY

It is simply a matter of logic

There is a *dichotomy* between those who understand the fourth word in this sentence and use it correctly and those who do not. The latter are in the great majority, since, like other technical terms of logic that have suffered a similar fate, *dichotomy* is being popularized as a vogue word. The intention of those who have picked it up loosely is to dress their discourse with learning. The effect is the reverse. On Radio 3 the other day somebody introduced a piece of music with the words: 'At this time Dvořák had reached a serious *dichotomy* in his life: should he do so-and-so or such-and-such?' The introducer presumably selected the word because it sounded more impressive for the Third Programme than turning-point or some synonym. But by misapplying it, and underlining his misapplication with the adjective 'serious', all he achieved was the exposure of his ignorance of the word.

Dichotomy is a precise technical term of logic, astronomy, and botany, derived from the Greek words meaning cutting in two. It is the division of a whole into two parts, otherwise binary classification. In logic it means the division of a class into two groups that are mutually exclusive or opposed by contradiction. For example, everything must be either red or not-red. A strict *dichotomy* can always be attained by using the negative in this way; but then it labours under the defect that the species classed under the negation are left indefinite. If there are three sub-classes each exclusive of the other two, they are called a *trichotomy*.

The *Dichotomy* is the name of one of Zeno's paradoxes. Zeno of Elea, the pupil and friend of Parmenides and inventor of dialectic, set up in philosophical business by drawing pairs of contradictory conclusions from the premises of his opponents. For example, he argued that everything must be infinitely large, as follows. Either a thing has no size, in which case it is nothing, or it has size, in which case it can be divided. But the parts resulting from this division must either themselves lack size, and so be nothing, or have size, and so be further divisible. Therefore we must end with nothing or with infinitely many parts. If these infinitely many parts lack size they cannot contribute to the whole; but if they have size, however small, the whole they form will be infinitely large.

A somewhat similar paradox is put more vulgarly in the couplet:
'Great fleas have little fleas upon their backs to bite 'em,
And little fleas have lesser fleas, and so *ad infinitum.*'

The *Dichotomy* is one of his paradoxes used as arguments for the impossibility of motion. It is a variant of the more famous Achilles and the Tortoise. Space and time are taken to be continuous. Achilles gives the tortoise a start in a race. He takes at least some time to reach the tortoise's starting-line, by which time the tortoise has sprinted a little way ahead of this line. So Achilles has now to make up this new, reduced lead. But by the time he has done this, the tortoise has once again got a little bit further ahead. Every time Achilles catches up with the tortoise's last starting point, that pesky chelonian has crept a little farther ahead. So Achilles never catches the tortoise. He whittles down its lead, but never whittles it down to nothing. The tortoise wins the hundred metres, the marathon, and any race you care to suggest. Achilles retires to sulk in the changing-room. The *Dichotomy* is a variant paradox, in which the fallacy also consists in dividing a distance into an infinite and therefore endless series of stages.

From this original meaning of *dichotomy* in logic the word came into astronomy to mean the phase of the moon or an inferior planet in which just half its disc appears illuminated. Aristarchus, the father of the heliocentric hypothesis, gave a method of determining the distance of the sun by the moon's *dichotomy* or 'half-moon'. In botany and zoology it is a form of branching in which each successive axis divides into two, known also in the jargon of the sciences as repeated bifurcation. It is especially common in seaweed and liverworts. In genealogy *dichotomy* means the forking of an ancestral line into two diverging branches. Family trees like the botanical sort sometimes observe *dichotomies.* American medical men, even more wanton jargonauts than their British counterparts, use *dichotomy* to mean fee-splitting by doctors.

From its meaning in logic *dichotomy* has been widely and avidly adopted into common parlance to mean differentiation into two contrasting or sharply opposed groups; for example, practice and theory, good and evil, written and spoken evidence. That is a perfectly respectable and intelligible derivative use. But from there it has been kidnapped and dragged along less respectable paths to mean anything divided into two or resulting from such a division; and thence to mean something paradoxical or ambivalent. For many people it is now the word that comes inevitably to mind when they wish to express difference, conflict, clash, wide gulf, division, cleavage, and similar concepts. It does not mean what they want it to mean; and any of those other words is better used to describe such distinctions as those between faith and reason, science and poetry, the Communist and the non-Communist world. When somebody recently wrote in *The Times*: 'Was there an awful *dichotomy* on her part when he finally decided to retire—a mixture of sadness and relief?', the only logical answer was: 'Er, no, since you put the question that way there cannot have been.'

15/ DILEMMA

A dilemma without horns is a poor cow

Fashionable misuse has dehorned the dilemma, so that the poor cow is becoming as bare-headed as a Red Poll. To use *dilemma* as if it were a learned synonym for a difficulty, or, colloquially, a fix, or a jam, impoverishes the language by spoiling a useful word.

Dilemma is primarily a technical term of logic and rhetoric derived from the Greek words meaning a double proposition or premise (lemma). It means an argument that forces one's opponent to choose between alternatives each unfavourable to him. The Romans called this an *argumentum cornutum*, an argument with horns, either of which will impale the victim. In logic a *trilemma* is a three-horned argument: a state of affairs or syllogism of the nature of a *dilemma*, but compounding three alternatives instead of two, as indeed there can be. The notion that, because it is derived from Latin *alter* (one or other of two), alternative cannot properly be used of a choice between more than two possibilities is a fetish.

The technical description of a *dilemma* in logic is hypothetico-disjunctive: that is, a hypothetical syllogism having a conjunctive or conditional major premise and a disjunctive minor (or one premise conjunctive and the other disjunctive). A *dilemma* is a form of argument designed to show that something, usually unpleasant, will follow either if a given assumption is true or if it is false. It should be distinguished from an *antinomy*, a contradiction between two assertions for each of which there seem to be adequate grounds; and a *paradox*, which is a single, unacceptable, and often self-contradictory and absurd conclusion for which there are seemingly irresistible grounds.

The classic example of a *dilemma* from the classical world is the Athenian mother who says to her son: 'Do not go into politics, my boy. For, when you become a politician, if you do what is just, men will hate you; and if you do what is unjust, the gods will hate you.'

The odious child rebuts her *dilemma* with the obvious retort: 'On that argument I ought to go into politics, mother. For, once I become a Member of Parliament, if I do what is just, the gods will love me; and, if I do what is unjust, the electorate will love me.'

From this technical use *dilemma* has acquired a respectable, popular, and non-technical meaning. In this secondary meaning it implies a choice between two (or, loosely, several) alternatives, which are or appear equally unfavourable. For example, a shop can reasonably be said to be faced with the *dilemma* of whether to lower prices or accept fewer sales. The Host of the Garter Inn in *The Merry Wives of Windsor* has persuasive grounds for saying that he is 'here, master doctor, in perplexity and doubtful *dilemma*'.

Morton's Fork was a kind of historical *dilemma*. Henry VII's ingenious and successful Chancellor caught tax-payers and would-be tax-avoiders in a *dilemma*. If they appeared poor, his inspectors said that anybody who lived so frugally must have something saved for a rainy day; and isn't it funny how it suddenly looks like rain? If they were big spenders, his inspectors said that they must have plenty of money to spare, because it was seen in their port and manner of living. English tax-payers were impaled on the horns of a *dilemma*. King Henry died rich.

The nautical version of this popular sort of *dilemma* is to be between the devil and the deep blue sea, or, originally in the seventeenth century, the dead sea. The devil was the caulker's name for the seam in the upper deck planking next to a ship's waterways. No doubt they gave it that name because there was very little space to get at this seam with a caulking iron, making it a particularly difficult and awkward job. The caulker was in a popular *dilemma* between the devil and the deep blue sea, since there is only the thickness of the ship's hull planking between this seam and the sea.

The kitchen cabinet version of a *dilemma* is to step out of the frying-pan into the fire. The woodman's version of a *dilemma* is to be in a cleft stick, which is a tight spot in metaphor as well as in the forest. This phrase was originally colloquial, but has been a standard and useful piece of English for the past two centuries. It is an example of a useful cliché, that is one that conveys a meaning more concisely and exactly than any other form of words.

By what Fowler described as slipshod extension *dilemma* is now widely used to mean something like a common-or-garden predicament, with no notion of the particular choice between two evils inherent in the word. An example of this use is: 'the modern *dilemma*: what to do to spend all this time.'

To rob *dilemma* of its horns in this way deprives it of its unique properties as a word, and weakens the language to the detriment of all who speak it and write it. *Dilemma* should be used only when there is a pair, or at any rate a definite number, of lines that might be taken in argument or action, and each is unsatisfactory. The thing to remember about a *dilemma* is that it is a wilder beast to hold by the horns than a wolf by the ears.

16/ DIMENSION

The difficulty of measuring a new dimension

Most of us find it hard enough to make sense of a three-dimensional view of the world, without bending our minds with a fourth, fifth, or further *dimension*. Accordingly, our present modish enthusiasm for figurative extension of *dimension* is confusing as well as pretentious. We use it as a convenient word-of-all-trades, when 'feature' or 'factor' would be simpler.

In the archaic days of Euclidean geometry, space was agreeably simple. *Dimension* comes from the Latin *dimetiri*, to measure. Not surprisingly, therefore, in English it originally meant the action of measuring or a measurement: 'Accordynge to the ordinarie accoumpte and *dimension* which the pylotes and cosmographers doo make.' This meaning is now obsolete.

Dimension then came to mean measurable or spatial extent of any kind, as length, breadth, thickness, area, or volume. Milton catalogued these *dimensions* grandly in *Paradise Lost*, when the gates of hell are opened on ancient chaos:

'A dark Illimitable Ocean without bound,
Without *dimension*, where length, breadth, and highth,
And time and place are lost.'

A *dimension* is one of the three coordinates of position. Thus, a line has one *dimension*: length. A plane has two *dimensions*: length and breadth. A cube or other solid body has three *dimensions*: length, breadth, and thickness. The fourth *dimension* could be described by a bold poetic metaphor as time, and was so described.

In algebra a *dimension* is a term for the unknown or variable quantities contained in any product as factors. Thus x^3, x^2y, and xyz are each of three *dimensions*. If a situation can be mathematically described by specifying n numbers independently, then the

mathematicians say that the totality of possible situations has *n*
dimensions and the situation has *n* degrees of freedom.

Over the past century these tidy meanings of *dimension* have
been complicated by two opposing tendencies. Scientists such as
Einstein, finding Euclidean explanations of space insufficient, have
pioneered new, difficult, and very precise *dimensions* for space and
other matters. Non-scientists, unluckily, have adopted very imprecise figurative uses of the word.

The new scientific extensions of *dimension* are not explicable in
a short essay, and not intelligible by this writer of short essays at
any rate. We must take it on trust that a *dimension* can now mean
to a physicist the number of elements in a basis of a vector space.
Let us not go deeply into the *Method of Dimensions* or *dimensional
analysis*.

In this new technical sense *dimension* means the power to which
any one of the fundamental quantities or units is raised in the
expression defining a derived quantity or unit in terms of them.
These 'fundamental quantities' are usually taken to be mass,
length, and time, sometimes with the addition of one or more other
quantities, such as electrical and magnetic phenomena. Let us turn
pale, and leave the scientists to their own *dimensions*, where, no
doubt, they know what they are up to.

In non-scientific discourse *dimension* has been widely adopted
and adapted. It has been used figuratively for three centuries: 'The
Expedition against Hispaniola; the *Dimensions* of this great Prep-
aration vastly exceeding the difficulties.' 'The passion for athletics
which in Oxford has now almost reached the *dimensions* of a
mania.'

It is now used to mean the particular set of circumstances within
which someone or something exists. It is used to mean one of the
planes of organization or one of the aspects of a cult phenomenon
(the definition is Webster's), as in, 'Every situation has environmental, organic, and social *dimensions*.' It means the range over
which or the degree to which something extends, as in the vast
dimensions of a disaster. It means the quality, character, or moral
or intellectual stature proper to or belonging to a person. It means
lifelike or realistic qualities, as in, 'Hamlet emerges bloodless,
without *dimension*.' It means largeness of vision or thought, as in,
'His work has a *dimension* lacking today in the plays of lesser men.'

A guided weapon described as 'a significant new *dimension* in
ground force defence' means a significant new factor. 'Artists and

laymen have considerably different semantic *dimensions* in their responses to modern art' means that they use different words to express those responses.

However, in spite of these wide extensions, the word attained new *dimensions*, you might say, if you favoured the metaphor, recently. In *Music Weekly* on Radio Three a critic said of Miklos Rozsa that his music for films had added 'a totally new *dimension* to his stature as a composer'. This extravagant use of the muddled metaphor magniloquent indeed adds a new *dimension* to both *dimension* and stature. The juxtaposition of *dimension* and stature used figuratively wakes the literal meaning in each, and reminds us incongruously that the Hungarian composer in Hollywood is not a man of exceptional height.

17/ DOCTOR

*The art of medicine consists of amusing the
patient while Nature cures the disease*

Until recently the general public regarded the medical profession
with healthy scepticism, as being quite as likely to kill them as to
cure them. *Si monumentum quaeris, circumspice* would be equally
applicable as a sermon on the grave-stone of a general practitioner
buried in a country churchyard. But as long as men are liable to
die and want to live, a doctor will be made fun of, but he will be
well paid. Now our modern superstition, fear of disease and death,
and lack of spiritual security have turned our doctors into medicine-
men and magicians. Accordingly, we no longer make fun of
doctors. And the title *doctor* is being abused by being confined to
its medical connotation and endowed with supernatural overtones
of guru, confessor, and hierophant.

When Dr David Owen was appointed Foreign and Commonwealth Secretary in the British Government in 1976, the
comment was widely made that he was a real *doctor*, unlike
some other Members of Parliament who called themselves *doctor*.
Presumably the reference was to Dr Rhodes Boyson and his
fellow PhDs.

This comment was wrong. *Doctor*, from *docere*, to teach, was
originally a teacher: one who, by reason of his skill in any branch
of knowledge is competent to teach it, as in the *Doctors* of the
Church, certain early fathers distinguished by their eminent learning, so as to have been teachers not only in the Church, but of the
Church. For about five centuries the two most common uses of
the word *doctor* were to designate: either any recognized medical
practitioner, however qualified; or a person who, in any faculty or
branch of learning, has attained to the highest degree conferred by
a university. This latter title originally implied competency to teach

76

the subject in which the *doctorate* was held. *Doctor* of Philosophy (PhD, or, at Oxford, DPhil) is the commonest of these, as it marks the satisfactory completion of apprenticeship in research in any subject. In Britain there are specific *doctorates* in medicine (MD or DM), science, and many other faculties.

In a paradox that puzzles foreigners and would alarm the patients if they realized, most medical practitioners in this country are not *doctors*. They do not have any university *doctorate*, because this is an extra research degree taken some years after the qualifying bachelor's degree (MB), which licenses a *doctor* to prescribe dangerous drugs, sign death certificates, and perform the other mysteries of his trade. Others qualify as *doctors* by an equivalent examination to the MB from such non-university bodies as the Society of Apothecaries, and the Royal College of Physicians and the Royal College of Surgeons. Perhaps newly qualified house officers should not yet be called *doctors* (except that this would scare the lives out of their patients), because they are not fully qualified medical practitioners until they have performed the compulsory one year of jobs before registration.

The qualifying label differs throughout the world. In North America all medical practitioners take an MD as the qualifying examination. In Britain none do, although those who qualify earn the honorary and colloquial title of *doctor*. This causes transatlantic confusion. A British Bachelor of Medicine and Doctor of Surgery will be asked 'Are you MD?' by an American who wants to find out his background. In British medical jargon MD can also mean 'mentally deficient'. The British surgeon, having been introduced as *doctor*, replies no to both MD questions, and so misidentifies himself to the questioner as non-medical. Surgeons add to the confusion by calling themselves Mr or a female equivalent, even when holding a university *doctorate*; but that is another story. When the knighthood arrives, professional identification becomes impossible. The British use titles as camouflage rather than identification. In the circumstances, to call a British medical practitioner by the wrong title is a venial slip. Those who mind don't matter, and those who matter don't mind.

The difficulty is due partly to there being no single word in English that corresponds, for example, to the German *Arzt* or the Swedish *Läkare*, and identifies exclusively a medical practitioner. Shall we go back to *leech*? *Physician* will not really serve, because in Britain this generally means the type of *doctor* who is not a surgeon, radiologist, and so on, and who usually holds an additional qualification from the Royal College of Physicians.

We are missing another word to denote what a physician specifically practises, as a surgeon practises surgery, and a radiologist practises radiology. The root word Physic is never used except in Regius Professor of Physic, and this is too easily confused with Physics. In Britain we sometimes use Medicine, which is ambiguous, since the same word has also to cover the whole craft of healing, as in *Doctor* of Medicine or medical student. In North America they maintain the century-old influence of Austria and Germany by using Internal Medicine as a translation of *Innere Medizin,* and may call its practitioner an internist. This in its turn can be confused with intern, who in Britain is a house officer.

The verb *to doctor* has come down in the world while its noun has been going up. Accordingly one *doctors* the cat, or a company's accounts, but not a patient unless one wishes to frighten him. And who will *doctor* Dr Who?

18/ ELITISM

All animals are equal, but some animals are more equal than others

Élite, and its frenchified siblings, *élitism* and *élitist*, have recently come rapidly down in the world. Our society is neurotically egalitarian in general principle, if not always so enthusiastic in private practice, when the equality is applied to us personally. Bernard Shaw was an exception among *anti-élitist* egalitarians in advocating a strict equality of incomes. He was depressingly typical of them in his inflexible refusal to set an unselfish example by giving up his own very substantial, and therefore on his own account very unjust, *differential* above the average national income. *Élitist*, like bourgeois, paternal, academic, and fascist, has been leached of most of its descriptive content, and turned into an emotional and propagandist anathema *contra diabolos*.

At the same time as the depreciation of *élitism*, *differential* in the sense of an *élitist* difference in wages between one class of workmen and another, especially between skilled and unskilled workmen, has come up in the world. Groups as diverse as university teachers and miners complain about the erosion of their *differentials*, and campaign to have them restored. The miners tend to be the more successful. In other words they are claiming, many of them correctly, to be *élites* (though they might not care to be so counted, because of the new emotionally negative overtones of the word). *Anti-élitists* proclaim that all men are equal. If they go on to claim their *differentials*, they are declaring that some are more equal than others.

Élite, in its modern sense of the choice part or flower of society, or any body or class of persons, crossed the Channel into English early in the nineteenth century. Byron indicated its recent arrival by quarantining it within inverted commas in *Don Juan* (1819-24):

'With other Countesses of Blank—but rank;
    At once the "lie" and the "*élite*" of crowds.'

The same word, *elite*, but without the acute accent and pronounced in an Anglo-Saxon way, had been in the language for at
least six centuries, and is now obsolete. It came directly from Old
French, and was used: as a verb, to mean to choose or elect to
office; as a past participle, to mean a person chosen, specifically a
bishop elect; and, as a noun, to mean an election. For example of
the first of these, *The Destruction of Troy* of *circa* 1400 has: 'Of
his daughters one Creusa was called that Aeneas afterward *elit* to
wed.' We might as well give up the accent, which is a nuisance,
now that the word is thoroughly at home again in English. However, it will be many years before it loses the whiff of Gauloises and
garlic in its pronunciation.

Foresters use *élite stand* to describe one selected for seed collection on account of its specially good quality. In the same woody
jargon an *élite tree* is one selected for seed collection or for veg-
etative propagation on account of some specially good quality it
may possess. *Elite type* without the accent is a standard size for
letters used in typewriting, measuring horizontally twelve letters
to the inch.

Élitism, as a philosophy or policy, has been widely adopted in
modern political and sociological jargon to mean advocacy of or
reliance on the leadership and dominance of an *élite* in a society,
or in any body or class of persons. Plato, in *The Republic,* is still
the most brilliant propagandist for an *élitist* government in a closed
society. Such totalitarian systems of government as communism and
fascism practise *élitism* by the dictatorship of the party. Lenin had
the fundamentally undemocratic conception of a narrow Communist Party consisting of an *élite*, whose more highly developed
class consciousness enables it to see farther than those among whom
it works. Not unnaturally, those left in the cold outside such *élites*
are envious and resentful, and feel that they too should be allowed
a say in their government.

But, *pace* our modern devaluation of the word, not all *élitism*
is wicked or undesirable. The word is allied to excellence. To pick
the England football team at random from the population, instead
of by the *élitist* method of selecting the best players, would be a
poor way of doing it; though, come to think of it, such a random
eleven could hardly do worse than some recent England sides.

Not all of us are capable of being opera singers, or astronauts, or international gymnasts, or nuclear physicists. It is absurd and lunatic not to be *élitist* in picking people for such demanding professions. Lord Todd, President of the Royal Society, said recently: 'In these days of rampant egalitarianism our concern for an *élite* in science may be regarded by some as outmoded. But in science the best is infinitely more important than the second-best. A country that ignores this or forgets it does so at its peril.'

There is a strong case for the *élitist* opinion that we should be governed by the wise and public-spirited, rather than the stupid and self-interested. However, it is important to retain the emergency power (not allowed in Plato's ideal republic) of getting rid of the rascals, when they turn out not to be as wise or disinterested as they pretended. In spite of its bad name, *élitism* is natural and desirable in many human activities. Luckily, if you look closely and positively at any human being, you can find special qualities that make him or her a member of some *élite*. We are all *élitists* under the skin.

19/ ENVIRONMENT

*It compasseth my path and my lying down,
and is acquainted with all my ways*

The *environment* is all around us, linguistically as well as physically.
The Department of the *Environment* has not only blotted the
landscape of London with its three giant matchboxes on end in
Marsham Street. It has also blotted the language by giving official
recognition to one of the woolliest vogue words of our time. In the
old days Government departments were named after what you
might call concrete objects such as housing and public works. The
environment is a conveniently hazy and pretentious cloak for the
generally harmful activities of ministers and bureaucrats. The Department of the *Environment*, the ugliest building in London, is a
suitable name for the department of state charged with the orderly
despoliation of the *environment*.

Environment arrived in English in 1603 to mean the action of
environing or the state of being environed, in the way that the
heavens environ the earth: 'I wot not what circumplexions and
environments.' In a speech to Parliament in the year of his death
Oliver Cromwell used the verb in this sense: 'You have accounted
yourselves happy on being *environed* with a great ditch from all
the world beside.' The words came originally from the French
environ, 'round about', and were related to *virer* and to veer.
Carlyle, that fitfully fuliginous and atrabilious tripudiator on short
Anglo-Saxon words when he could invent a frenchified polysyllable,
gave *environment* its modern meaning in the middle of the last
century. He is credited with the introduction of *environment* to
mean the objects or the region surrounding anything, as in:
'Baireuth, with its kind, picturesque *environment*.' This sort of
environment can now also be used to refer to the weather. 'The
environment is impartial' is a modern translation of the fuddy-
82

duddy King James's version: 'He maketh his sun to rise on the evil and on the good, and sendeth rain on the just and the unjust.'

Carlyle was also responsible for the less creditable first use of *environment* to mean the conditions under which any person or thing lives or is developed: the sum total of influences that modify and determine the development of life or character. He wrote, in a sentence that would not escape pruning by the fastidious sub-editors of *The Times*, who have to be thrifty with space to fit as much in as possible: 'In such an element with such an *environment* of circumstances.' In this sense of the word John Florio might have written, 'We are the creatures of our *environment*', if the word had been around in the early seventeenth century, and if he had not been such a lively writer. Instead he wrote, more pungently: 'Who sleepeth with dogs shall rise with fleas.'

In the past twenty years the *environment* has been widely taken up and loosely extended, both as a word and as a cause. Not before time, we have started to be concerned about the effect of man upon his *environment*. Man being the feckless and selfish beast that he is, this consists mainly of pollution and waste. People say things like, 'The general public can assert its constitutional right to a viable, minimally degraded *environment*.' And we applaud the vague sentiment, while deploring the imprecise language. The *environment* in this sense is like the weather: everybody complains about it, but nobody does anything about it. Indeed, the *environment* and the weather are often indistinguishable: 'Inside the rose-tinted, air-conditioned, *environment*-proof bulk reigned the modern architectural trinity, cleanliness, spaciousness, and luminosity.' A good *environment* is like *amenity*: everybody wants it, but nobody will pay for it.

So we have *environment* areas, controls, and ministers. We are told that the future pattern of cities should be conceived as a patchwork of *environment* areas of residence, commerce, or industry, from which traffic other than that concerned with the area would be excluded. In the jargon of the traffic planning industry, what an *environmental* area really means is a device for channelling motor traffic out of your street into someone else's, if possible three or four blocks away. There are man-made *environments*, or buildings, and, in the advertisements, engineering *environments*, or factories. To make their job sound exciting advertisers write, 'The *environment* is fast-moving and structured', and succeed in making it sound alarming. The successful candidate should wear a crash-helmet. There are *environmental* sciences such as meteorology, geology, and oceanography. The airline that advertises 'Eating in Soho will add to your total *environmental* experience' presumably means that there is nowhere quite like Soho; and quite right too.

A specialized use of *environment* in Phonetics means neighbourhood: 'The *environment* or position of an element consists of the neighbourhood, within an utterance, of elements which have been set up on the basis of the same fundamental procedures which were used in setting up the element in question.'

Environmentalism is a theory of the primary influence of *environment* rather than heredity on the development of a person or group, animal or plant. An *environmentalist* is: either somebody who believes in or promotes the theory defined in the last sentence; or, more commonly, somebody concerned with the problems of the *environment*, and especially with the effects of uncontrolled pollution of the earth's atmosphere. The latter is also described as an anti-pollutionist or a specialist in human ecology. Pollution is someone else's mess when it reaches you, as distinct from your mess when it reaches someone else, when it is called legitimate amenity effluent.

In the jargon of modern art, an *environment* is a work of *environmental* art: a form of art that encompasses the spectator instead of confronting him with a fixed image or object. *Environmental* art became popular in the 1960s, as the traditional concept of a work of art as an object declined. The trends were towards the involvement or participation of the viewer, and towards the integration not only of painting, sculpture, and architecture, but also of the visual arts with the other art forms. Viewers were invited to climb into and move works of art. In this sense an *environmentalist* means an artist who creates *environmental* art. One of them, called Tony Martin, tries to explain what he is up to: 'People become part of the art object. They score it. They compose it. I supply the format.'

As may be inferred from what has gone before, the word *environment* is now used to mean almost anything. Game-parks in the United States advertise that the visitor can see bears not, as we used to say in our old-fashioned way, in their natural surroundings, but in their *environmental* habitat. An aerosol of disinfectant announces enigmatically on its label: 'Kills most household germs on *environmental* surfaces.' As the Aberdonian said of the air frae the bagpipes: 'Beat that if ye can!' Presumably the manufacturers

84

of the aerosol are using the fashionable word *environmental* not to mean anything, but as a sonorous incantation; in the same way that advertisers of a brand of vodka trumpet fatuously: 'The Charisma of Cossack.' No Cossack that ever sat on horse has ever exhibited the slightest flicker of charisma, at any rate for the British drinking public; nor has any brand of vodka.

The London Borough of Camden has started putting up signs that read: '*Environmental* Area: No Through Route.' The curious lexicophile follows the signs, hoping to enjoy a park or open space of some kind. But the only distinguishing feature of the area marked by the signs turns out to be numerous blocks of council flats. Evidently the *environment*, which used to surround the residential area, has now become synonymous with it. Or worse, the word has been rendered quite vacuous, to be used by the pretentious for just about any area whatsoever. Such linguistic pollution is as bad in its way as the *environmental* sort.

20/ ESCALATE

A moving staircase of rhetoric
that travels only upwards

With luck the *escalation* of the vogue for using *escalate* and *escalation* to mean no more than any old increase in anything has halted. Let us now hope for a rapid *de-escalation* so that the new word can be confined to the meanings for which it was invented: the cold jargon of nuclear deterrence, and thence, figuratively, the hot jargon of wages and prices.

The words are a back-formation from escalator, the name invented for a moving staircase and derived from the Latin *scala*, a ladder. Escalade, from the same root, has been in the language of warfare since the sixteenth century, having been adopted from the French masters of siege warfare. As a verb it means to scale a wall or fortification. As a noun it means either the action of scaling the walls of a fortified place by the use of ladders, or the actual ladder used for this hazardous action. The *OED* described as erroneous a subsidiary use of escalade to mean a series of terraces one above the other, like a staircase.

There was no need for *escalate*. Escalade as verb and noun had long been in similar metaphorical use. But Sir Ernest Gowers judged the prospects of the two rival words correctly in his revised edition of Fowler's *Modern English Usage* in 1965: 'Escalate is likely to drive escalade out. It has the advantage of novelty and a more native look, and a moving staircase provides a more up-to-date metaphor than a scaling ladder.'

Escalate originally came into the language to mean to climb or reach by means of an escalator, or, intransitively, to travel on an escalator. *Granta* of November 1922 decorated the novel word with inverted commas: 'I dreamt I saw a Proctor "escalating", rushing up a quickly moving stair.' So vivid a new word rapidly

86

acquired figurative uses. As early as 1938 the *Kansas City Star* explained: '*Escalation* means the building of bigger battleships when other nations do so.' The fact that the *Star* thought that an explanation was necessary suggests that the use was new. As early as 1947 Hugh Dalton was telling the House of Commons that the report of the War Damage Commission advised a certain *escalation*.

But the words did not *escalate* out of the Underground into prominence until they were adopted by the jargonauts of thermonuclear strategy. The most articulate guru of them all, Herman Kahn, gave the authoritative definition in his book *Thinking about the Unthinkable* in 1962: 'There is a tendency for each side to counter the other pressure with a somewhat stronger one of its own. This increasing pressure step by step is called *escalation*.' Kahn constructed an *escalation ladder* of no fewer than sixteen steps leading from 'subcrisis disagreement' to the aftermath of 'all-out war', after which we are going to need more than a ladder to climb out. He explained: 'War by miscalculation might also result from the process called *escalation*.' A limited move may appear safe, but set in motion a disastrous sequence of decisions and actions. *Facilis descensus Averni.*

Although designed for thinking about nuclear warfare, *escalation* came into popular use during the non-nuclear war in Vietnam. Each time one side or the other introduced reinforcements or weapons not previously used in the war, the other side condemned the act as *escalation*. 'The President chose to begin with one of the less drastic options, leaving open the possibility of *escalation* to more violent ones.' The word got a bad name, because of the highly successful propaganda of the anti-war movement. Accordingly the American Administration preferred to talk of widening or increasing the war, rather than *escalating* it. Eventually Dr Martin Luther King called on his followers for 'an *escalation* of our opposition to the war in Vietnam.'

In real life escalators run both up and down. In its figurative use *escalation* runs only up. So *de-escalate* and *descalate* were introduced to mean the reverse of escalation, for example, the mutual reduction step by step of military activity.

Escalate is therefore a precise and logical word to mean to increase by successive stages, specifically to develop from conventional warfare into tactical 'nukes' and then on to global nuclear war. It looks silly and pretentious when used indiscriminately in less awesome contexts to mean no more than to increase or accelerate. The writer in the American magazine, *Horizon*, was aware of this pretentiousness when he wrote in 1963: 'The wish of the author to magnify or *escalate* (favourite new word in Washington) the importance of a trivial utterance by grandiloquent terminology.' *Escalation* is a suitable word to describe the development of conventional warfare into nuclear warfare, or the use of successively more powerful types of weapon in war. Hence it has been extended logically to describe any increase or development by successive stages, for example, of prices or wages, or from marihuana to hard drugs. Where there are no successive stages in the increase, *escalation* is wrong, and betrays its user as a parrot of fashionable clichés.

21/ EVANGELICAL

Give honour unto Luke Evangelist;
For he it was (the aged legends say)
Who first taught Art to fold her hands and pray.

Most *evangelicals* have a tendency and a zeal to be *evangelistic*. But by no means all *evangelists* are *evangelical*, which is used in English to refer to a special sort of Protestant. A useful distinction has been established between the two words. But now that the technical language of religion is no longer common parlance, the two words are often and increasingly confused. This is from a recent review of French language teaching on commercial television in *The Times Educational Supplement*: 'The teachers' notes are somewhat fuller, but a lot of space is taken up by an *evangelical* exposition which is likely to alienate users.' In November 1977 an article in *The Times* on Marxists in higher education accused Marxist lecturers of having a burning sense that they alone are right and, mysteriously, an *evangelical* desire to convert their students. For a second this conjured up the Groucho Marx image of these earnest academics having taken up not just the opium of the people, but a particular puritanical brand of the stuff.

In both examples the more usual words for spreading the gospel, whether literally or figuratively, would have been *to evangelize, evangelist*, and *evangelistic*. More potentially misleading because of its ecclesiastical context, an account in *The Times*, also in November 1977, of the General Synod of the Church of England reported that 'the Bishop of Winchester, Dr Taylor, was afraid lest Christians might reach for an *evangelical* crusade instead of facing such issues as class and race, industrial disputes and family relationships'.

As is evident, both words are derived from the same root, *evangelist*, the bringer of good news; specifically, one of the writers of the four gospels, Matthew, Mark, Luke, and John; and generally, somebody who preaches the gospel. In the New Testament the word is used three times of a travelling missionary, probably designating no special office, merely his activity and duty of proclaiming the gospel. For example, Philip was described as both a deacon and an *evangelist*, and the Apostles were said to have *evangelized*. In the third century the technical usage of *evangelist* to refer to one of the authors of the canonical gospels was established.

The word came to be used figuratively in secular contexts to describe somebody who spreads any opinion, belief, or doctrine, either by formal preaching, or by personal conversation, or by publishing manifestos. In this way it makes sense to say that the French Revolution found its *evangelist* in Rousseau; that Mary Whitehouse is the *evangelist* of cleaning up television; and that Colonel Gadaffi is an *evangelist* of revolution and associated turbulent activities in other men's countries, but not his own.

Evangelistic is the adjective of this noun, and accordingly means preaching the gospel or, metaphorically, spreading any opinion or belief. It is an appropriate term to apply to proselytizing Marxist lecturers or opinionated textbooks.

Since the Reformation *evangelical*, another adjective from *evangelist*, has been generally applied to the Protestant churches, because of their claim to base their teaching pre-eminently on 'the gospel'. This claim is of course disallowed by their adversaries, but, as with other self-assumed party names, the designation has received the sanction of general usage. *Evangelicals* allow church professionals less power to impose their interpretations of the gospel on the individual than other churches.

In the Church of England *evangelical* is the technical term for the Low Church party or school, which lays special stress on personal conversion and salvation by faith in the atoning death of Christ. This group originated in the eighteenth century to revive religion at a time when faith and morals were low, and many clergy were negligent and worldly. It had several points of contact with the Methodist movement; but it sought to work within the parochial system, and never contemplated separation from the Church of England. Opponents heartily disliked the religious earnestness, priggishness, and puritanical enthusiasm of the *Evangelicals*. In 1768 six *evangelical* undergraduates were expelled from St Edmund Hall, Oxford, for 'too much religion'. But the piety and humanity of the *Evangelicals* gradually won them a large following, and in the nineteenth century they took a prominent part in missionary work and social reform in such great matters as the abolition of slavery and the factory laws.

Evangelicals emphasize the preaching and personal acceptance of the gospel. They do not attach much importance to liturgical worship or church authority. They reject the doctrines of baptismal regeneration and the eucharistic sacrifice. In general, they exhibit a strong suspicion of the Roman Catholic Church, and strong hostility to characteristic Tractarian and High Church doctrines.

The words had a different history on the Continent. Germans, whose *evangelisch* has different connotations (all the Protestant Churches of Germany are designated '*Evangelische Kirche in Deutschland*'), tend to imagine that English *evangelical* churches are either simply Protestant or very inclined to missionary work. They are often wrong.

We live in an ecumenical and pagan age, and are cooler about these ancient religious parties. However, the man who uses *evangelical* as a metaphor for persuasive in secular contexts instead of *evangelistic* is stepping quite unnecessarily into deep and turbid ecclesiastical waters.

22/ FEEDBACK

Feedback offers food for thought

A weakness of popularized technicalities is that their popularizers get no *feedback* from the technical jargons, from which they have stolen the technicalities, to correct their imprecisions. Politicians, journalists, and other dealers in other men's ideas pick up a pretty word from academics, and start bandying it about in public, either to impress the spectators with their learning, or because they have not fully grasped the meaning of the term and are accordingly fearful of paraphrase.

The same process of misunderstanding and misappropriating other men's jargon occurs also within the academic world. Most of the physical sciences have built up exact technical jargons, well established and defined over the centuries, and capable of expansion and development; and, by the way, it is instructive to consider how long it took some of the sciences to accumulate adequate technical vocabularies. The terms used even by Newton seem quaint today; and many words now known exclusively in their scientific contexts had everyday origins in common speech.

However, a large and woolly region of academic study is still searching for its vocabulary as well as its identity. This region includes economics, sociology, 'political science', 'management sciences', demography, psychology, and every aspect of knowledge in which the human imponderable plays an important part. These disciplines lack the scientific rigour, the precise technical jargons, and indeed the discipline of the physical sciences. They might be described as *soft sciences*, since, if they are sciences at all, they are a different sort of science from such hard sciences as chemistry and astronomy, and from such deductive, analytic activities as mathematics and logic. Mercifully, these *soft sciences* can never attain the iron laws and rigid terminology of the hard sciences, because their subject, man, is an unpredictable, irrational, gloriously unmeasurable creature with free will and a soul, not simply a congeries of molecules and chemicals. The *soft sciences* mistakenly tend to envy the mathematical certitude of the hard sciences, and pinch their jargons, often with ludicrous results. We are at an early stage in the evolution of vocabularies of *soft sciences*, and earnest seekers after truth in them must be excused for pirating other men's jargon and putting it to the wrong use.

Feedback is a good example of this process. This learned-sounding word is constantly on the lips and typewriters of modish academics in the *soft sciences*, in contexts that make it clear that they mean no more than reaction, response to a stimulus, or merely information. The word is preferred because it sounds more scientific.

Feedback was invented for the hard sciences of electricity, radio, electronics, and computers. For their purposes it means the return of a fraction of the output signal from one stage of a circuit (or amplifier, etc.) to the input of the same or a preceding stage. *Positive feedback* tends to increase the input, amplification, etc.; *negative feedback* decreases it. In the early days of radio it was difficult to obtain sufficient amplification with the relatively expensive, bulky, and power-consuming valves then available. Consequently *feedback* was assumed to be of the positive or 'regenerative' variety, having the purpose of increasing the amplification. It therefore seemed very odd when H. S. Black published his concept of what he called 'stabilized *feedback* amplifiers' in *Electronic Engineering* for January 1934. But as the implications of the concept gradually became clearer, there was a sense of excitement that it is now hard to recapture. Interestingly, stabilizing *negative feedback* had in fact been used earlier in non-electronic contexts, notably by Pfund in an optical arrangement to increase the deflection of a galvanometer.

In regulatory systems *feedback* is used to compare output with some standard to be approached. *Negative feedback* is inherently stabilizing, because it decreases the error. *Positive feedback* is inherently destabilizing, and the error gains explosively in magnitude. In *The Fontana Dictionary of Modern Thought* (1977) Professor Stafford Beer of Manchester and Pennsylvania Universities cited the Watt steam governor as the classic example of *negative feedback*. In this a pair of weights attached to the engine shaft fly outward by centrifugal force if the engine tends to race. This movement operates a valve to reduce the supply of fuel. As an example of *positive feedback* Professor Beer suggests a 'growth economy'. In this, increased profitability is ploughed back in order further to increase profitability, a process which indeed becomes destabilizing in the limit.

In servo-mechanism language *feedback* is the signal that comes from measurement of the controlled variable *back to* the controller. For example, when a naval gunnery officer alters the bearing of a gun-turret by turning a knob, the servo-mechanism turns the turret; and the measurement of the actual bearing is relayed back to the controller for comparison with the required bearing. This is *feedback* in a hard science, or in a hard life, at all events.

There are now whole fields of knowledge, and whole branches of industry, concerned with the practical application of *feedback*. Cybernetics itself could be defined as largely the science of *feedback* and its applications. It is particularly galling for such precise specialists in *feedback* when their word, describing an exact and beautiful concept, is abused as a mere buzz-word.

Soft scientists, particularly those brutal *jargonauts* the economists, now use the word loosely to describe any transfer of any sort of information from anywhere to anywhere: backwards, forwards, port, or starboard. Simpler words would make their meaning clearer, and avoid the suspicion that they are trying to blind us with bogus science. But other words would lack the impressive ring of electronic certitude in *feedback*.

23/ GERIATRIC

Why such an unkind word for our elders and betters?

Other ages and cultures have respected and indeed venerated old age. Present society in the United Kingdom and especially the United States has made a golden calf of youth, and is consequently embarrassed by the subject of old age. We are terribly frightened of growing old and dying, and fall into periphrasis and euphemism when we try to talk about them. The Victorian middle classes were embarrassed by sex, or at least pretended to be so in public. They went to the absurd extremities of covering up the legs of their chairs, and referring to trousers, if they could not avoid the subject, as unmentionables. Accordingly, their swearwords were sexual, for swearing performs the cathartic function of shocking by saying the unsayable. Today, by repetition, familiarity, and their admission to the respectable as distinct from the slang and unconventional dictionaries, the explicit sexual words are losing their sting to shock. Before long at this rate the most shocking insults will no longer be sexual, but senile and moribund. Men purple with rage will find relief in screaming at each other that they are senile old ruins. The driver who considers that the collision was not his fault (by definition, any driver in any collision) will come out of his seat shouting: 'You putrefying old cadaver!'

We should treat old people better, if only for the unheroic prudential reason that we may one day grow old ourselves. But to call them senior citizens, though it is done from gentle motives, is a circumlocution worthy of the comfortable concentration camps for old people in Florida and California, where they are shut away from society as though the disease of age were infectious. It is a euphemism almost as chilly as saying that somebody has passed over, or passed on, or passed away.

And now there is a fashion for using *geriatric* as though it were a jocular and somehow less depressing synonym for old. *Geriatrics* comes from two Greek words meaning old age and 'relating to the physician', and means the branch of medicine or social science dealing with the health of old people. As the diseases of youth and middle age yield to medical treatment, so the diseases of the elderly come to be regarded as more important. The word *geriatrics* was coined in the *New York Medical Journal* of 1909 as the opposite of paediatrics. *Gerontology* is a related word meaning the scientific study of old age and the process of aging. It bears the same relationship to *geriatrics* as psychology bears to psychiatry.

Geriatric accordingly has a clearly defined and useful meaning as an adjective: concerned with the medical care of old people. But it is being widely misapplied as though it meant merely old, or very old, or tiresomely old, or amusingly old, because a long, learned word is felt to be less brutally precise than a common, short one. Cardinal Basil Hume, the Archbishop of Westminster, claimed in an interview on his appointment that he was a *geriatric* squash player. He looks a remarkably fit and healthy man. But possibly he can be given the benefit of the doubt, and assumed to have been using the word correctly. Perhaps the local paper that referred to *geriatric* high jinks at an old people's home at Maidenhead was using the word soberly and advisedly, and understood what it was saying. But when a motoring correspondent wrote the other day of a *geriatric* car battery, the time had come to cry: 'Hold, 'old enough.'

The worst insult to our elders and betters is to lump them all together as the old, as if they were suffering from some unmentionable disease. We are all suffering from that disease. It is called life. We commit the same insensitive offence by lumping together all different sorts of people suffering from different handicaps as the disabled, as if they were not really people at all. A symptom of this insensitivity is to ask the person pushing a wheel-chair, 'Does he take sugar in his tea?', as if the disabled person sitting in the wheel-chair had lost the powers of thought and tongue as well as locomotion.

Geriatric, and its more cumbersome derivative *psychogeriatric*, are neologisms of medical jargon, and useful adjectives. Their common and insulting use is not as jocular general adjectives, but as pejorative nouns, referring to old people who are physically and mentally ill. 'There was this dear old *geriatric* in the bed next to me' and 'It's very upsetting to see these *psychogeriatrics* at the day

96

centre; they should all be in hospital' are examples of this increasingly prevalent practice. The use of an all-embracing adjective as a substantive for a whole class of people betrays ignorance of or indifference to the range within that class, and the single term hides the number of sub-classes. 'The old' range from 65 to 107, and are scarcely a homogeneous class. Such insult by adjective is usually directed at groups who are unknown to the speaker: the blacks; the whites; the disabled; the deviant; the criminal; the alcoholic. However, such a use of an adjective may also be a mark of esteem, as in: 'Only the brave deserve the fair.'

Most old people have common characteristics, such as low income, immobility, and lack of political clout to impress their views on party politicians. Nevertheless, we struggle to find an acceptable, apposite, and friendly name for them, when we need to refer to them as a class. 'Old-age pensioners', abbreviated to OAPs or pensioners, is considered working-class. 'Old folk' is regarded as patronizing. 'Senior citizens' never caught on in Britain, though it fared better in the United States. And 'the old' and 'the elderly' have become the most popular descriptions by default. They are not satisfactory for the reasons stated. The 'Cleveland housing for the low-income elderly project' opened in Ohio in 1977. Although by all accounts an admirable and humane place, it does not give that impression by its name. It sounds like a ghetto for sub-humans suffering from two incurable and infectious diseases. It would be kindlier nomenclature to revive the venerable substantive 'elders', with its biblical connotations of wisdom and reverence, to describe our elders.

Alan Coren, editor of *Punch* and a prince of television critics, reviewed the BBC production of *La Dame aux Camélias* of Dumas fils in 1977. He wrote with characteristic style: 'While the white camellia is hoisted, Marguerite Gautier goes through the *Almanach de Gotha* like a scythe, relieving *geriatric* Paris of around 7,000 francs a month, and this was in 1852 when you could go to Boulogne for the day, have a slap-up meal, and still get change out of five sous.' Strictly speaking, it was Marguerite's activities, I suppose, not Paris, that should have been described as geriatric. Such daring transference of epithets is part of the armoury of a shining wit. Those of us who do not write as well as the editor of *Punch*, almost all of us, would do well to think twice before writing *geriatric* outside a medical context, and find a more suitable word.

24 / IRONY

Life's little ironies are generally quite unconscious

Journalists suffer from a specific form of word block or writer's cramp known as intro trouble. It consists of procrastination and inability to decide on the introductory sentences of their pieces, even though the deadline is approaching ever nearer, and the sub-editors are baying hungrily for copy. So they day-dream of a magic telephone service that will automatically supply them with a first sentence so compelling that it will zap the chief sub-editor into a flicker of animation, lead the page, and grab the reader's attention by the scruff of the neck. *Ironically* is one of the most popular introductory words supplied to hard-pressed scribes by Dial-an-Intro, that invaluable but elusive Post-Office information service.

There is no shred of *irony* in its popularity, only haziness. *Ironically* is evidently used for all these meanings:

1. by a tragic coincidence
2. by an exceptional coincidence
3. by a curious coincidence
4. by a coincidence of no importance
5. you and I know, of course, though other less intelligent mortals walk benighted under the midday sun
6. oddly enough, or it's a rum thing that
7. Oh hell! I have run out of words for starting a sentence with$_x$

Study of modern newspapers suggests that meanings six and seven are becoming by far the most common. This is a shame, because it devalues a useful word.

Irony is a figure of speech in which the intended meaning is the opposite of that expressed by the words used. It generally serves for sarcasm or ridicule, in which laudatory expressions in fact imply

98

condemnation or contempt. Old grammarians used to call it, charmingly, 'the dry mock'. *Irony* is addressed to an imagined exclusive inner circle who are in the joke, while profane outsiders who are being mocked are mystified. It is by definition an élitist form of speech. Lord Macaulay, in his essay on Bacon, cited as an example a drayman in a passion calling out, 'You're a pretty fellow', without suspecting that he was uttering *irony*. It was sarcastic *irony*, especially in a religious age, to note Dante's intimacy with the Scriptures, and add, 'They do even a scholar no harm.'

Irony comes from the Ancient Greek word for dissimulation. The Greek tragedians used *dramatic irony* as one of their most powerful tricks. Their audience knew their plots as well as British children know the plot of Cinderella and the words of the latest jingle of commercial television. But the characters in the play, Agamemnon, Oedipus, and the rest, were in the dark about the fate that was waiting for them round the next corner with a blunt instrument; or, in Agamemnon's case, a sharp, two-handed one. The audience got a delicious thrill from foreseeing the future, and understanding the meaning hidden in sentences pregnant with doom.

So when Clytemnestra, persuading Agamemnon to display the sin of hubris by walking into his palace again over a Welcome Mat of purple tapestries, says: 'With the help of the gods, my unsleeping vigilance will take care of everything else in the way that fate ordains', a frisson of horrified expectation ran through the audience. They knew what the dragon queen had in mind, and the chorus had an ugly suspicion, even though Clytemnestra's pompous turkey-cock of a husband could not see what was behind the bathroom door. Purple bathmats are unlucky as well as impious. Producers of horror films, farces, and pantomimes still use this sort of *dramatic irony* visually, when they make us, the audience, aware of something nasty that is pulling damnable faces and creeping up behind the back of the heroine, who is unaware of its approach. In *dramatic irony* there is a surface meaning for the dramatis personae and an underlying one for the spectators, who enjoy the ancient pleasure of being in the know.

Socratic irony was the rather irritating trick by which Socrates professed simple ignorance about any question that came up for discussion. His underlying point was that no dogma should be accepted without question; everything should be carried back to first principles. Modern judges are employing a debased form of *Socratic irony* when they ask questions like: 'What is a Garbo?

What are Sex Pistols?' Socrates was one of the original *eirons* in Greek; an *eiron* was the foxy dissembler who said less than he meant, whose words were pregnant. 'He personates an unlearned man, and is an admirer of others as wise', as if butter would not melt in his mouth. The innocent *irony* of Socrates was a powerful masked battery.

Accordingly, the dogmatists plunged in with pity or contempt to enlighten his ignorance. And those who had heard Socrates argue before sat back to enjoy the *irony* of his leading the opposition gently up the garden path, and turning conventional wisdom inside out with simplicity. Again with *Socratic irony* there is the double audience: insiders (Socrates and his friends, who know their Socrates) and outsiders, about to step into it.

From these two primary Greek meanings of *irony* we have derived our modern idea of the *irony of fate,* or what the French call *ironie du sort.* This postulates a double audience again. Most of the world expects things to go on happening normally, as they have in the past. But an inner circle of *cognoscenti,* to which, of course, we and our readers belong, share the joke with fate, which has a banana-skin in the road around the next corner waiting to send the uninitiated flying. This is the fickle finger of fate: a contradictory outcome of events, as if in mockery of the promise and fitness of things. Ignorant and uncomprehending outsiders are taken by surprise. Fate shares her amusement with us, the elect, knowing élite, who are aware that what happens is the unexpected, that just when life seems to be running smoothly it is going to turn round and bite us in the ankle.

In the jargon of literary criticism the classifiers assert that there are two principal categories of *irony*: situational and verbal. Both sorts again depend for their effect on a double audience, on the exploitation of the distance between either events or words from their contexts.

An example of the situational *eiron,* the dissembler who says honey words with stings in their tails, and in his person brings two conflicting and contrasting worlds into sharp focus, is Jeeves. On the surface he is the obsequious gentleman's gentleman. But he knows, and we know, and even Bertie Wooster occasionally and hazily suspects, that he is not the servant but the master, who twists Bertie around his little finger. Pope's *The Rape of the Lock* is a brilliant essay in verbal *irony,* contrasting the high-flown style of the verbal couplets with the banal and mysterious subject.

'What dire offence from am'rous causes springs,
What mighty contests rise from trivial things!'

Ironically is a powerful and explicit word. It is being weakened by use as an all-purpose introductory word to draw attention to every trivial oddity, and often to no oddity at all. *Ironically* those who use the word in this way are its worst enemies. The *irony of fate* has become a hackneyed phrase. We are all so knowing these days that we all expect the worst, and are seldom disappointed.

Did Lady Louise meet her Waterloo
in the little girls' room?

Euphemism, the use of a mild or vague or periphrastic expression as a substitute for blunt precision or disagreeable truth, is common to most languages. The word comes from the Greek for to speak fair. The figure of speech consists in the substitution of a word or expression of comparatively favourable implication or less unpleasant associations, instead of the harsher or more offensive one that would more precisely designate what is intended. The very name reminds us that cautious euphemism prompted the Greeks to call the Black Sea the Euxine (the hospitable one) in the hope of averting its notorious inhospitality, and the Furies the Eumenides (the good-natured ladies) in the vain hope that they might be flattered into being less furious and more merciful.

The Hebrew word for the Lord, YHVH, rendered into English as Yahweh or Jahveh or Jehovah, is one of the oldest four-letter words under taboo in history. It is known in Greek as the Tetragrammaton, *the* four-letter word, and is still never spoken or written by a pious Jew.

Euphemism enables the furriers to sell skunk's fur under the sweeter-smelling name of Alaska Sable. Totalitarian states make assassination sound better by calling it liquidation, and aggression by calling it liberation. What used to be called bluntly Labour Exchanges became Employment Exchanges, and are now JobCentres. The poor are described as the underprivileged or the lower income brackets. To make sense, lower-income should be hyphenated, but never is. Poor nations are described as developing ones, in a triumph of hope over experience. We do not die, but pass away, or on, or over, or go west. There is kindness as well as deceit in some euphemism.

Litotes, the form of meiosis or rhetorical understatement that replaces the positive notion required with its opposite and a negative, is used as a form of euphemism. When a Civil Servant describes a case as by no means uncomplicated, what he means is that Einstein would have taken a day and the rest of us would take a year to unravel it. George Orwell recommended that we should inoculate ourselves against litotes by memorizing the sentence: 'A not unblack dog was chasing a not unsmall rabbit across a not ungreen field.'

God, sex, and death (the creator of life, the beginning of life, and the end of life) are the principal breeding-grounds and habitats of euphemism in English. This is evidently not so in all cultures. Bronislaw Malinowski discovered that the Trobriand Islanders during the 1914-18 war had no inhibitions about talking bluntly to him about sex, or indeed performing the act, in public. But they had a taboo on the private and dangerous activity of eating in public, or discussing the subject. Euphemism about God gave English the host of medieval swearwords that distorted the unmentionable holy name, as in Zounds, God's wounds. Euphemism about sex prompted the Victorians to call such fundamental garments as trousers inexpressibles or unmentionables. Euphemism about death gives us most of our funebrial vocabulary, including cemetery itself, which is the Greek word for a dormitory.

The most prolific single source of euphemism in English is not God, sex, or death; but, perhaps an offshoot of the English attitude to sex, what is euphemistically described as answering a call of nature. The French are less mealy-mouthed. Their notices say *Défense d'uriner*, where ours say (mysteriously and disquietingly to a foreigner) 'Commit no nuisance'. We have invented a lexicon of names for the same useful piece of domestic furniture: jakes, privy, latrine, water-closet, W.C., lavatory, convenience, ladies, gents, toilet, powder-room, cloaks, little girls' (boys') room, comfort station, rest room, the basement (American, because that is where it tends to be), the head (nautical), the John. Bolton Royal Infirmary displays a fine notice: 'Diabetic patients are to be toileted on arrival.'

Loo is the latest and most fashionable euphemism in British English for privy or lavatory. Words to do with excretion have a proclivity to euphemism in most languages, because most cultures

103

have a taboo, or at any rate feel embarrassed, about performing the acts in public. Lavatory itself is a euphemism. You do not go there principally in order to wash your hands, and there are still plenty of them where you cannot do so anyway. The coy, colloquial *loo* has a mysterious etymology. Some suggest that it is a Cheshire Cat of a pun, in which all but the smile has faded away from Waterloo. James Joyce, that paronomasiamane, specifically made this full pun in *Ulysses* (1922): 'O yes, *mon loup*. How much cost? Waterloo. Watercloset.' The derivation from Waterloo cannot be demonstrated more rigorously.

Other suggested and equally unpersuasive etymologies are: from the French *l'eau*, and particularly the old Scottish warning shout like fore (taken like much Lallans from the French; cf. ashet) as they emptied their chamber pots out of a top-storey window, *gardy-loo*; and a modification of the French *lieux d'aisance* (public conveniences or almost comfort stations). There is even a suggestion that *loo* is a misreading of the French euphemism of putting numéro cent, 100, on the lavatory door in a hotel, in order to avoid embarrassing sensitive guests who wish to relieve themselves. In this whimsy, an Englishman on a visit to France read the number 100 as *loo*.

Professor Alan Ross has an appropriately U etymology. He has discovered a well-authenticated story of a practical joke that took place at Vice-Regal Lodge, Dublin, when the first Duke of Abercorn was Lord Lieutenant of Ireland in the decade after 1866. Each bedroom door had a card on it with the name of the occupant. Somebody changed the cards round, and the card of a certain Louisa or Louise, called *Lou* for short, ended on the lavatory door. She must have been Lady Louise Hamilton, who died in 1940. Ever afterwards the family and friends called the lavatory the *lou*.

Nancy Mitford first popularized *loo* in her books, and it was evidently originally U (upper class). It is now common in spoken and even written English. In an open letter to Nancy Mitford Evelyn Waugh stated that toilet was 'pure American', and that lavatory was the British euphemism. Americans dispute this, or say that things have changed since he wrote.

Lavatory is the most neutral general word in British English, though it has an uneasy history. It started life in the fourteenth century (from the Latin *lavare*, to wash), meaning a bowl for washing. Then it came to mean the ritual washing of the priest's hands before he celebrated Mass; thence an apartment for washing
104

the hands and face; and finally, in the nineteenth century, such an apartment with a water-closet.

Toilet (from the diminutive of the French *toile*, cloth) originally meant a cloth wrapper; then a cloth cover for a dressing table; then the dressing table itself; then a lady's dress; then a dressing-room furnished with bathing and washing facilities, including (though do not shock us by mentioning it) a water-closet. Hence toilet has acquired its most common meaning of a plumbing fixture, usually of porcelain though sometimes of stainless steel, equipped with a mechanism for flushing with water and used for defecation and urination. It nevertheless retains its connexion with its obsolete meaning of women dressing, so that a painting entitled *Venus at her toilet* sounds possible but odd. Toilet is used in British English, but it is a twee genteelism, non-U, and felt to be an Americanism.

The most interesting vulgar term, described by the *OED Supplement* as coarse slang, is crapper. Popular etymology, as usual apocryphal, asserts that the name originated from an English plumbing manufacturer called Crapper, who invented the useful piece of furniture. To crap, coarse slang for to defecate, is said to be a back formation from the legendary Mr Crapper, but there is nothing to substantiate this folk etymology. It has pupped crap-house, crapping case, crapping castle, and other familiar names for the dunny or earth closet; as well as the American verbs to crap or talk nonsense, to crap around or behave foolishly, and to crap out or be unsuccessful. Americans also shoot craps, that is, play the game of craps with dice. Crap is also used in the singular for the losing throw, and for the game itself.

Water-closet is technically accurate, and respectably old (1755), but sounds pedantic. Its abbreviation W.C. sounds old-fashioned. Jakes and privy were splendid but are obsolete. Ladies and Gentlemen as signs on public lavatories are being replaced by Women and Men, as a gesture to the classless society. Pub jocularities such as Mermaids and Divers are despicable; and so is the Americanism Powder Room or Little Girls' (Boys') Room. John and head are unknown in Britain, except in American writing and films. Washroom is an even wetter euphemism than lavatory. Bathroom makes foreigners wonder why the Briton or American, who wishes simply to relieve himself, should wish to take a bath after a meal. British hostess to foreign guest: 'Would you like to wash your hands?' Foreign guest: 'No, thank you. I washed them on your front doorstep before I rang your bell.' Lavatory is the pick of a poor bunch.

But the quest for a euphemism in such lavatory matters is a will-o'-the-wisp. Each new word rapidly becomes as explicit as its predecessors, and has to be replaced. Call it what you like, we know what you are up to in there.

26/ LOVELY

We have become lovely and
pleasant in our thank-yous

Everything not merely in the garden, but also in the pub, the shop,
the bus, the street, and all the other meeting-places and talking-
shops of life, is suddenly *lovely*. Pay for a purchase, buy somebody
a drink, give up your seat to somebody else, and the odds are a
hypermarket to a television-dinner of fish fingers that she or he
thanks you by saying: 'Lovely.' An elderly and distinguished public
figure who had not caught up with the idiom was surprised when
he telephoned *The Times* with a death notice in 1978:

Public figure: 'Good morning. Are you the one who receives the
           notices of births, and deaths, and so on?'

Tele-ad girl, for it is she: 'Yes.'

Public figure: 'Good: I've got a notice of death for you here.'

Tele-ad girl: 'Oh, *lovely*.'

Half-way through dictation, public figure: 'I hope you are noting
    the punctuation as I give it to you, for that is how it is to be,
    and not necessarily as your compositors think it ought to
    be.'

Tele-ad girl: 'Right—*lovely*.'

At the end, public figure: 'Send the bill to me, please.'

Tele-ad girl: '*Lovely*.'

Public figure, in a gloss on the conversation: 'I hasten to add that
    no feelings were hurt, or anything stupid like that. My feelings
    were a mixture between amusement and groans at what is
    happening to our language.'

   People used to express their casual gratitude by 'thank you',
'thanks', or 'ta'; with 'luv', 'deary', or (in Glasgow) 'hen' tacked
on the end as an optional extra, depending on the region in which
the thanking was being done. In the past year the popular word for

trivial thanking has suddenly become *lovely*. Like much raging slang it is odd and crass.

Alasdair Aston, the poet, anticipated this idiom in a darkly witty poem of 1970 called *Everything in the Garden is Lovely*:

> 'Even the fat slug
> That drags its belly nightly
> Over dank paving
> And into the heart of the lettuce
> Is *lovely*.'

The poem goes on to catalogue things found in a garden and not usually considered lovable, from wireworm to viper's bugloss, and proclaims that they are all *lovely*. Even the gardener, who has fallen flat on his back, dead, is *lovely*:

> 'The *lovely* flies walk in his *lovely* mouth.
> Everything in the garden is *lovely*.'

How can *lovely* have so suddenly come to mean thank-you? It is too new a usage to have been noticed by even the most recent lexicographers. *Lovely* started its life in Old English as an adjective meaning loving. No less an authority than King Alfred used it as an adverb to mean affectionately. Malory used it to mean amorous.

Then the slow semantic erosion of the centuries wore away the amorous connotations, and the word came to mean 'delightful', or 'excellent', as a general term expressive of enthusiastic adulation. So by 1653 Izaak Walton's *Compleat Angler* could say to his contemplative friend: 'Come let's to supper. Come my friend Coridon, this Trout looks *lovely*.'

There the word rested without major development until the middle of this century, when we gave *lovely* an absolute or substantival sense to mean a *lovely* creature, usually, in the male chauvinist 1930s, a female. The earliest authorities cited by the *OED Supplement* are Auden and Isherwood: 'It (sc. the working class) prefers our larger and livelier organs of enlightenment, which can afford snappier sports news and bigger photographs of bathing *lovelies*.' Dylan Thomas in *Portrait of the Artist as a Young Dog* wrote: 'I missed the chance of a lifetime, too. Fifty *lovelies* in the rude and I'd left my Bunsen burner home.'

This *lovely* noun as smasher has no obvious connexion with *lovely* as thanks; unless the extravagant supposition is made that at some time in the late 1960s shop assistants and bus drivers en masse started chatting up their female customers by addressing them as bathing-beauties. *Lovely* ('ta'; 'that's *lovely*'; 'how *lovely*')

108

seems to have started life as a response for some slight service rendered: for example, giving exactly the right money for something bought in a shop. Now it has grown and weakened to become an automatic response to any money being handed over, whether precisely the right amount or not.

In *The Duchess of Duke Street* (a television serial based on Rosa Lewis, the generous and extravagant matriarch of the old Cavendish Hotel) in 1977 Mrs Trotter (Rosa) asked an American staying at her hotel during the 1914-18 War if brandy would suit for the offered drink. He replied: *'Lovely'*, with a loud crash of anachronism that offended the sharp ear of Roy Fuller, as well as the ears of others who care for such things.

Such vogue silliness usually has a fast and furious life, and dies young of over-exposure. Oh, Wouldn't it be *Lov-er-lee* if such a fate were to overtake *lovely*! It would make a *lovely* corpse. Farewell, my *lovely*.

27 / MATRIX

Magna ista scientiarum matrix

Some words are born pretentious (ongoing ambience, or, if you fancy the French spelling, ambiance). Some words achieve pretentiousness (situation). And some have pretentiousness thrust upon them (charisma, parameter). The last class consists principally of technical terms from the academic and industrial worlds misappropriated and carelessly misapplied by ignorant outsiders. The user's intention is to clothe his discourse with spurious learning, and blind his readers and auditors with fashionable science. His achievement is to hang out banners on the outward walls of his prose to warn all who read or listen to waste no more time reading or listening.

Matrix is a conspicuous warning signal. A supposed expert at a symposium on river ecology the other day gave fair warning to his audience when he spoke repeatedly about 'the brown trout *matrix*'. What he ought to have meant, if he was using the word strictly in its algebraic or logical sense, was an orderly array of the coefficients that his colleague was presenting separately. Unfortunately his other words made it clear that what he actually meant was the little brown fish in person, in river or loch.

Matrix is a typical new popularized technicality. It has a number of precise specialized meanings in several sciences, near-sciences, and pseudo-sciences. It sounds eminently impressive. It can be supposed to have a conveniently hazy general meaning, derived from its etymological connexion with *mater*, the Latin mother, as something within which something else originates, or takes form, or develops. And it is a safe bet that nine out of ten of those who drop the word plonkingly into their unspecialized discourse would be embarrassed if asked for an exact definition.

Matrix has so far acquired no fewer than eleven separate special-
110

ized meanings, the most important coming from the precise disciplines of logic and algebra, and from the technologies of computers and radio electronics. Its original meaning, now obsolete, was as a synonym for the uterus. And it retains a number of related physical meanings of organs from which others grow. Its dominant modern meaning comes from mathematics, from which it has been adopted by other disciplines that envy the precision of mathematics. In maths a *matrix* is one of a class of rectangular arrays of mathematical elements (such as the coefficients of a set of simultaneous equations, or the components of a set of vectors) that are subject to special algebraic laws. In logic a *matrix* is an array of symbols representing truth-values, giving the result of all possible assignments of truth-values to components of a propositional form. It is another name for a truth-table, that useful little instrument of arraying the total truth possibilities for investigating the interrelations of necessity, truth, possibility, and falsity. This use was pioneered by Alfred Whitehead and Bertrand Russell, the founding fathers of modern mathematical and logical philosophy; for example, *Principia Mathematica*: 'Let us give the name of *matrix* to any function, of however many variables, which does not involve any apparent variables.' In Chomskyan linguistics a *matrix* sentence is that one of a pair of sentences joined by means of a transformation that keeps its essential external structure and syntactic status. In 'the book that I want is gone', 'the book is gone' is the *matrix* sentence.

On, bravely on, from abstractions to technologies that we can see and touch. In computer jargon a *matrix* is an ordered table or two-dimensional array of variables for use in computer programming. 'Cores are usually built together to form square or possibly rectangular *matrices* in which each *matrix* contains as many cores as there are words in the memory bank. Most *matrices* nowadays contain (64 x 64) 4,096 cores.'

In broadcasting a *matrix* is a circuit designed to accept a number of inputs and produce outputs that are linear combinations of them in different proportions. *Matrix* mechanics is an alternative formulation of quantum mechanics that does not involve a wave function, devised by Werner Heisenberg in 1925.

In addition *matrix* has specialized meanings in geology, typesetting, coining, phonography, dentistry, photography, the study of fungi, and the terminology of the coal industry, to name but a few. A need is clearly felt for *alma matrix* in these technical jargons,

111

because it does a job that cannot be done so succinctly by any other word in the vocabulary. But when somebody uses the word outside its jargons in general speech, it is a strident warning to listen suspiciously, because somebody may be showing off.

There is nothing wrong with a word acquiring several alternative uses and meanings. Consider how well the ubiquitous and useful little word 'fly' has done for itself in collecting meanings. A rule of first come first served for words and meanings would be absurd. It would emasculate Shakespeare, and give us a literature in which all metaphors had been expurgated as illegitimate. The objection is to using a useful word with so little regard to its meaning that it becomes meaningless, as in the brown trout *matrix*.

You could say, if you were that way inclined, that the advertisements of estate agents are a *matrix* of amazing English. The *Wolverhampton Express and Star* published a fine specimen in 1977: 'Come and behold! Here is the most breathtaking re-creation of character-living imaginable. Three-bedroom bungalows and houses wed traditional lure and modern chic in a scintillating synthesis of sovereign elegance. Exposed beams, bow windows, rustic fireplaces, illuminated alcoves, antique doors, floral-tiled bathrooms, dramatic kitchens, built-in almost everything. PLUS endless thoughtful extra touches like Georgian style garage doors . . .' Character-living is presumably what the psychotherapists describe as role playing. In a dramatic kitchen the fridge plays Mussorgsky's *Night on the Bare Mountain* and sends up rockets when you open its sovereign elegance. A thoughtful Georgian garage door is one that takes its time before it allows itself to be opened. The housing estate does not seem to be a *matrix* in which one could feel at home.

28/ MODULE

I am the very module of a modern misconception

Modules are modish. The man who lets them drop with a splash in his prose informs his audience or readers that he is *au fait* with the latest clichés of modern thought. He may not convey much else, however, except, of course, esteem for his trendiness. *Module* is a term of architecture that has been widely and loosely adopted as a metaphor by less concrete sciences and technologies, and even beyond them. For those of us who tend to trip over our *modules*, here follow the principal modern uses of the word.

1. A standard or unit for measuring: 'Many of the ancients served themselves with ordinary grains of corne (which *module* hath also entred our English Laws) for the Measures both of length and capacity.'

2. In architecture: a standard unit of measurement used to create proportional relationships between parts and the whole. For example, in the classical orders, the semidiameter of the column at the base of the shaft is the *module* or unit of length by which the proportions of the parts are expressed: 'The height given to the column is fourteen *modules*, or seven diameters.'

3. Hence, in the building industry: a length chosen as a basis for the dimensions of parts of a building to facilitate their coordination, so that all lengths are an integral multiple of it; specifically, a *module* of 4 inches (101.6 millimetres). Buildings planned in this way are described as *modular*. Almost all building needs some form of dimensional coordination. This need becomes acute in prefabrication, for which the use of the *modular* principle is particularly appropriate. 'Houses of the future may all be built using a four-inch cube called a *module* as the structural atom.'

4. Hence, still in building: one of a series of production units or

component parts that are standardized to facilitate assembly or replacement, and are usually prefabricated as self-contained structures. 'Our housing needs in the next nine years must be met with factory-built *modules*, assembled on site.'

5. By analogy from building: a standardized part of a piece of furniture and especially of transistorized artifacts such as telephone exchanges and switchboards. 'The *modules* are bolted together to form a full machine ready for final trouble-shooting.'

6. In astronautics: a *module* is a unit of an aircraft or spacecraft that has a specific function, and is often designed to function apart from the main craft as a self-contained, self-supporting unit. 'A capsule was to be fired from the earth into orbit round the moon, when a special part of it, christened the lunar excursion *module*, would detach itself.'

7. In Computerese: one of a number of distinct, well-defined units from which a computer program may be built up, or into which any complex process or activity is analysed (usually for computer simulation), each of which is complete in itself but bears a definite relationship to the other units. 'The computer programmer breaks his problem down into *modules* and gives the *modules* names so that they can be handled.'

8. In educationalists' jargon: a unit or period of training or education. The adjective *modular* is also popular in the new education jargon. For example, the Welding Institute is offering '*modular* courses in welding engineering: the basic course will consist of three full-time residential *modules* as shown schematically below'. The illustration in the Welding Institute's brochure shows nothing more formidable than three boxes containing details of the curriculum. 'Eventually the sort of retraining envisaged could fit in with the notion of periodic training *modules*, whereby skilled men would take repeated periods off productive work to renew their perhaps rusty skills and learn new ones.'

9. In mathematics (hold tight; not for beginners): originally a set that is a subset of a ring and is closed under addition and subtraction; now usually defined as a commutative additive group whose elements may be multiplied by those of a ring, the product being in the group and the multiplication obeying the associative and distributive laws. Selah. 'A *module* is a mathematical set that is a commutative group under addition

and that is closed under multiplication which is distributive from the left or right or both by elements of a ring and for which $a(bx) = (ab)x$ or $(xb)a = x(ba)$ or both where a and b are elements of the ring and x belongs to the set.'

10. In engineering: the pitch diameter of a gear wheel in millimetres (or inches) divided by the number of teeth.

11. In printing design: a box. The layout of *The Times* in the 1960s became *modular* (organized in little boxes) instead of linear (more flexible, less pretty).

12. In fashionable unspecialized discourse: a class, group, or thingum-a-jig that sounds good but is difficult to define precisely.

A recent advertisement was using meaning number 12 when it declared: 'Practical involvement in management training is essential, and exposure to presentation of financial *modules* would be an added advantage.' Presumably financial *modules* mean accounts; and what is being asked for is somebody who has had experience of presenting accounts. The advertisement manages to make accountancy sound a dashing and slightly dangerous activity. At *The Times* we hold occasional meetings between people interested in the same subject; what you could call, if you were that sort of verbal hijacker, an interface of those with common parameters. These meetings were originally and coyly called *modules*. Then, by a combination of confusion and frivolity among the hacks, they became nodules. Now they are called noodles, which sounds agreeably and aptly like thick soup.

29/ MOMENT IN TIME

You know, I had to pause for thought, didn't I?

Nature abhors a vacuum. Television and radio producers, creatures far removed from Nature, abhor the very idea of silence. It does not matter much to them what is being said, so long as their precious air is full of noises. The worst thing that you can do in a live broadcast is to dry up. However, few human beings other than Samuel Johnson and Bernard Levin have ever been able to speak continuous good sense without stopping at frequent intervals to consider what they are going to say next. The alien atmosphere of a broadcasting studio, with its complicated machinery and ostentatiously bored technicians, is conducive to stage fright, stuttering, and aphasia.

This may be one reason for the popularity among the broadcasting classes of cotton-wool phrases that have sound but no meaning. They issue from the mouth automatically and without thought, occupying time, and so giving the speaker a moment to work out what he is going to say next. An example may be the crass '*at this moment in time*'; as in: 'The usual stuff about meaningful confrontations taking place *at this moment in time*.' People use this phrase because they suppose, mistakenly, that it sounds more impressive than the plain 'at this moment', the fancy 'at the present instant', or the pitiful monosyllable 'now'. They evidently feel that the longer tautology invests their words with dignity and importance, when all that it in fact does is to expose them as pompous and illiterate. But a subsidiary advantage may be nothing more than that *at this moment in time* takes longer to say. It fills this moment in time with effortless, bland noise, and so gives the speaker a brief pause during which he can select his next platitude. If you do not mind being rude, the thing to do to anybody who says *at this moment in time* in your presence is to hold your hand up, insist on

116

interrupting, and ask: 'With what sort of moment other than one in time are you making a distinction, pray?'

Other sorts of moment have recently become popular. There is *not for a moment*, meaning emphatically not. The man *of the moment* is of importance *at this moment in time*. *Never a dull moment* is a catch phrase designating constant variety. It first occurred in J. K. Jerome's *Three Men in a Boat*, but Eric Partridge, the learned arbiter of such matters, says that it became a naval catch phrase during the last war. It is used sardonically in moments of excitement or danger, but also humorously in moments of personal, incidental stress, as when one's leave has been cancelled for some usually unexplained reason. *To have one's* (or *its*) *moments* is to be impressive on occasions. *To live for* (or *in*) *the moment* is to live without concern for the future. The *moment of truth* (from the Spanish *el momento de la verdad*) is the final sword-thrust in a bull-fight, so much enjoyed by Hemingway.

'Y'know', '*You* know' with an incongruously heavy stress on the 'you', and 'I mean' are three other very popular meaningless locutions much in vogue to pad out abhorred silence on the wavebands. Every other broadcast sentence seems to end with one of these Selahs; and if it does not end with it, it begins with it, and uses it at all intermediate pauses. As well as the cotton-wool qualities of these phrases, their popularity is also due to the modern British cult of inarticulateness, which considers it bad form and élitist to sound dogmatic, didactic, or even definite about anything.

Another very fashionable piece of pseudo-working-class idiom that is all the rage in broadcasting is the trick of attaching a 'didn't I?' to the end of every statement. 'I went and asked him, didn't I? I had to do something, didn't I?' This use may be yet another meaningless noise to avoid silence and give a pause for thought.

The perverse stresses and emphases that broadcasters misplace on 'the' before a consonant, on pronouns, and on other normally unstressed syllables may be misguided attempts at dramatic effect. They may be pure ignorance. They may be broadcaster's *borborygmi*, nervous mispronunciations induced by the awful atmosphere of a broadcasting studio, which is the human equivalent of a goldfish bowl. They may, on occasions, be attempts to protract sound in order to give time for thought. However, sometimes what the speaker actually said was 'the . . . er . . .', and paused to hunt

117

for his next word. He correctly put the stress on 'the', because the next word 'er' began with a vowel. The editor then made it sound odd by snipping 'er' and its surrounding pregnant silences off the tape. Producers hate ers almost as much as silence.

*The pendulum of the mind oscillates
between sense and a nonsense,
not between right and wrong*

No one is exempt from talking *nonsense*: the misfortune is to do it solemnly. The concretion of *nonsense* to mean a particular piece of *nonsense* is now complete and solid. It has become unfashionable to describe something as *nonsense*, or a piece of *nonsense*. People call it, concretely, *a nonsense,* with the indefinite article. By this new use they mean a muddle or a fiasco, especially in the phrase *to make a nonsense* of something. Denis Healey is only one of a number of public men who deploy *a nonsense* throughout their speeches *passim.* They appear to mean by their designation of something as *a nonsense*:

1. I disagree with that
2. I do not understand that

or 3. I understand that only too well, but do not wish to enter into argument about it, because my position is indefensible, and I know that I should lose the argument. On occasions the silly-billies contrive to combine all three meanings. The learned fool writes *nonsense* in better language than the unlearned, but it is still *a nonsense.*

When, where, and why *nonsense* got its article is a puzzling little linguistic question, but not beyond all conjecture. The primary meaning of *nonsense* is evident from its appearance. It means that which is not sense: spoken or written words that make no sense or convey absurd ideas. It also means absurd or senseless action. From the beginning it has been used also exclamatorily as an interjection to express disbelief of, or surprise at, a statement.

Even in the salad days of its use, when it was green in misjudgment, *nonsense* was occasionally particularized and given an article. Pope, in a letter of 1711, wrote: 'How easy it is to a Caviller to give a new Sense, or a new *Nonsense,* to any thing.' An even earlier example of particularized *nonsense* (1643) is: 'Every new *nonsense* will be more acceptable than any old sense.' Neither of these is exactly the modern non-idiom. By his *a new Nonsense* Pope meant 'a meaning that has no sense'. A sentence of 1655 is slightly nearer to the modern use: 'He understood not French very well, nor I his Fustian Language, so our discourse was *a* perpetual *Nonsense.*' This is still not quite the modern use, as exemplified in: 'The Government cannot give way to the railwaymen without making *a complete nonsense* of its pay restraint policy.' Sir Ernest Gowers described this use as unidiomatic: 'The idiom is *make non-sense* (or *make sense*) of something, without the indefinite article.'

The *OED* described the particularized use of *nonsense* to mean a piece of *nonsense* as obsolete. An example closer to the modern non-idiom (or, *pace* Sir Ernest, idiom) was written by Walter Scott in a letter of 1803: 'I daresay I shall go on scribbling one *nonsense* or another to the end of the chapter.'

The language has moved on since the *OED* published its fascicle N (William Craigie, 1907) and Gowers revised Fowler. In spite of these few early specimens of *a nonsense,* the phrase seems to have become widely fashionable only recently. The period appears to have been that of the 1939 war; and the dialect group that originated the use, the Army. The evidence for this assertion is admittedly thin, but quite persuasive. The two earliest citations for the new vogue use of *a nonsense* that volume 2, H-N, of the *OED Supplement* could find came from *Put Out More Flags* by Evelyn Waugh, first published in 1942. 'Everyone said, "Lyne made a *nonsense* of the embarkation;" ' and later, ' "It was all rather *a nonsense,*" said the subaltern, in the classic phraseology of his trade which comprehends all human tragedy.'

Waugh indicates that the use was Army slang. If he was correct in stating that it was classic phraseology, that might imply that it had been current jargon in Army messes for some time. If so, no earlier record of the usage has been preserved.

An interesting suggestion is that *a nonsense* is a continental European misuse of English idiom, being a literal translation of *ein Unsinn,* which also means, secondarily, folly and madness. After Hitler seized power, many refugees escaped to Britain, some of them speaking better English than others to start with. Witnesses who were around at the time remember such refugees saying: 'It

120

makes *a nonsense.*' It is suggested that such comical misusages were repeated at parties and in pubs, as a sort of in-joke. 'And soon those native English people not sensitive to, or interested in, the idiomatic use of English took up *a nonsense,* without intending to raise a laugh.' Others have suggested that American academics who spoke better German than English translated *ein Unsinn* verbatim, in the same way that they mistranslated *hoffentlich* to provide the new meaning for hopefully ('it is to be hoped') that is so ragingly popular that it is hard to imagine how some people managed English before it was invented. An American origin seems improbable, since almost all the examples of *a nonsense* are British.

The most likely guess is that *a nonsense* was imported by German refugees in the Thirties, and picked up by fashionable young subalterns, originally as a joke. Ever since then we have been using the phrase with increasing and modish frequency, until in the past year or two it has become a fad. *A nonsense* has a certain colloquial breeziness. It means muddle or cock-up rather than the original non-sense (Eric Partridge attributes *cock-up, circa* 1925, also to the Army, which seems to have an alarming need for words meaning this). If you mean the original *non-sense,* without connotations of absurdity and fiasco, you are prudent to write it with its hyphen. Edward Lear's *non-sense* is not vacuity of sense; it is a parody of sense, and that is the sense of it. 'Is this a question?' is a *non-sense* question. An undergraduate at Oxford got his First in philosophy in spite of having answered that non-question with the single sentence: 'No, but this is an answer.'

A nonsense, like rubbish, has recently spawned its intransitive verb, *to nonsense,* meaning to talk *nonsense. A nonsense* uses one more syllable than the old idiom approved by Gowers of describing things simply as *nonsense.* It has become a fashionable cliché. It is not incorrect, but it is in danger of becoming *a nonsense* and a laughing-stock itself. Note J. K. Galbraith's idiomatic sarcasm: 'It is a far, far better thing to have a firm anchor in *nonsense* than to put out on the troubled seas of thought.'

31 / NO QUESTION

To question or not to question, that is the bee

The image of a fat banker slithering down the Cresta Run without a toboggan was unwittingly evoked in an avalanche of metaphor in a piece of City journalism recently: 'The market was shaken by a sudden plunge in the pound's exchange rate, and as no floor was provided by the Bank, at least at first, there was a snowballing effect.' Like most jargons, the private language of the money market slips easily into absurdity. Such technical terms as plunge, floor, and snowball are presumably dead metaphors for those who use them in their hermetic daily 'shop'. For us outsiders they are still very much alive, and are roused by chance collocations to mental motion-picture shows as ludicrous as the Keystone Kops.

There is *no question* that such sectional vocabularies are rich sources for resurrection of metaphors as surprising as Lazarus's. There is *no question* that the third and fourth words in this sentence constitute a fashionable phrase. The air is full of confident *no questions* being used to hustle dubious statements and arguments past audiences too slow or too polite to object. There is *no question* of our being able to stop the nuisance, which will have to live out its busy but brief life as a vogue expression, until all of us have grown tired of it.

But *no question* has the notable eccentricity of being fashionable with two opposing meanings simultaneously. At times it is used to mean the same as 'no doubt'. At other times it is used to mean almost the opposite. In a single issue of *The Times* in 1977 trumpet-tongued Bernard Levin was sounding off about there being *no possible question* that Michel Guérard had succeeded in his principal endeavour, which was to make non-fattening food not merely palatable but delicious. Meanwhile on the Arts Page the editor of *Punch* had a double-barrelled *no question*: there was *no*

122

question that the makers of a television programme wished to make our flesh creep; *no question,* either, that they did so. Whereas, on yet another page a spokesman for the West German Government was reported as having told a press conference that there was *no question* of any large-scale publication of the official volume documenting the Schleyer kidnapping and Lufthansa hijacking.

It is a rare Janus phrase that can manage to look in two so nearly opposite directions without getting a stiff neck. The idiom is that *no question that* means no doubt that, and *no question of* means no possibility of. But the two distinct meanings are sometimes confused, and often confusing.

At any rate, one old vexed question about question has been resolved. When *questionnaire* was imported from France earlier this century (too recently to be included in the original *OED* fascicle on 'Q' published in 1904; in the 1933 *Supplement* the first example of its use is dated 1901), purists complained that it was an unnecessary Frenchified immigrant. Fowler himself wrote that it was a pity that we could not be content with our native *questionary,* which is quoted by the *OED* from the sixteenth century. Commentary, glossary, dictionary, and vocabulary, with many less common words, would keep it in good company. Others said that if we did not adopt the perfectly good English word *questionary,* we should at least stigmatize the French intruder by pronouncing it in a Frenchified way, as *kestionair.* Usage has ignored the prescriptive purists, as it usually does. The influence of pollsters and government departments, which preferred *questionnaire,* has proved irresistible. *Questionnaire,* pronounced in an Anglicized way, has established itself as a useful native, and is quite at home.

We do well to English our pronunciation of immigrant words. The English are bad at foreign pronunciation. Sir James Murray once referred to the word 'Renaissance' in a lecture. After touching on the facial acrobatics and adenoidal and strangulated noises that most people found necessary in attempts to deliver the word in French, he exclaimed: 'Why don't they say Renassanss and have done with it?' In *Grand Larousse* the first meaning of *questionnaire* is given as a torturer or clerk who sets down the replies of the person tortured: a vivid metaphor for those unanswerable and interminable *questionaries* that Civil Servants torment us with.

There is *no question* that *leading question* is still widely misunderstood and misused outside its jargon, the Law. It is a question that suggests to a witness the proper or expected answer that he

123

is to make. Counsel are not allowed to lead their own witnesses to the answers they want from them by putting *leading questions*. There is *no question* of many outsiders understanding this. They take *leading* to mean principal, or shrewd, or intended to lead them up the garden path. So, when a direct or embarrassing question is put to them, they protest fatuously and meaninglessly: 'That is a *leading question.*'

Not on your nelly

Not to make a mountain out of a molehill (though what else is most writing?), but have you noticed that the previously inoffensive little adverb *not* is getting ideas above its station? It has recently acquired an imperative force, perhaps partly by ellipsis, but also with a negative verbal flavour contained within its simple little monosyllable of its mere motion. This is particularly noticeable in the vogue colloquial phrase: '*Not to worry.*' This modish and jaunty little expression leaps from a thousand pairs of lips every hour; and every hour it sounds a little less jaunty and a little more jaded. It is a hard phrase to construe. Are we to suppose that some such phrase as 'I tell you' or 'You are' has been omitted by ellipsis before '*not to worry*', to give the sense 'Do not worry?'

The *OED Supplement* cites George Eliot in *Middlemarch* as the grandmother of the usage: 'And he objects to a secretary: please *not* to mention that again.' This is a slightly different use. *Not* has indeed got a certain imperative force here, but some of the verbal load is carried by 'please'. *Not to worry*, with the naked and un-supported imperative in *not*, seems to have come into fashion in British English, though not American, since the last war.

The *OED Supplement* gives the earliest citation after *Middle-march* to the *Daily Mail* in 1958: '*Not to worry.* By the time he had finished with me I'd be doing long division.' Since then it has become a popular parrot cry; and because of its popularity irritates those who allow themselves to be irritated by popular catch phrases.

Not to worry has produced a litter of derivative expressions that also use *not* as a funny sort of imperative. A '*not* to bother; I'm going down to the country this evening' has been spotted. And there are records of a sighting of that rare and delightful variant: '*Not* to be overcome, son.'

The origins of imperative *not* are wrapped in agreeable mystery. After the original version of this essay first appeared in *The Times* more than fifty people wrote offering the true and only origin. Their suggestions ranged eclectically from the Latin *noli* followed by the infinitive to such Continental imperative infinitives first recorded by Thomas Cook as *nicht hinauslehnen* and *ne pas se pencher au dehors*. All claimed to have heard the phrase spoken long before the earliest written examples recorded by the *OED* (except for the rather different use in *Middlemarch*; and there may even have been one or two who claimed to have heard the phrase before *Middlemarch*, published in 1871-2). The weight of their evidence, in numbers as well as persuasiveness, suggested that *not to worry* was born during the last war, probably in the Royal Air Force, and possibly in Italy.

There were even earlier citations, which were charming, though unpersuasive. There was a music hall jingle of the 1920s:

> '*Not to worry*, not to flurry,
> Not to fret nor fume.
> Nothing good is got by worry
> In the happy month of June.'

A song of the 1930s included the lyric:

> 'When you see that aunt of mine,
> Be sure and tell her
> *Not to worry*
> If I'm late home.'

The latter is agreeable, but not to the point, since its *not to worry* does not stand on its own, but is dependent on the preceding imperative, 'tell her'.

The largest group of correspondents pointed to Italy during the last war. British servicemen picked up and brought home such mongrel phrases of dog Italian as *Ciao for now*. It is suggested that *not to worry* is a literal translation of some such colloquial Italian phrase as *non preoccuparti* or *non ti occupare*. Several remember obliging Italian civilians, when asked to do something, replying with such words as: '*Not to worry*, Signor Capitano, I fix.'

Another school attributes the phrase to the jokes of cynical and homespun philosophy introduced by the proem 'Confucius he say', as: 'Confucius he say rape impossible, because girl with skirt up,

126

she run faster than man with trousers down, eh?' In this version the complete saying went: *'Not to worry,* or if to worry, *not to worry* unduly.' Others say that it was not cod Chinese, but Arabic. Servicemen stationed in Iraq during the last war assert confidently that *not to worry* was a literal RAF translation of an Arabic word, which did duty for a shrug of the shoulders, and was in common use by the locally employed staff on airfields and bases in that part of the world. Others assert equally confidently that it originated in the South African Air Force during the last war, and that it should have an interrogative *eh* on the end, as, *not to worry, eh*? It was one of a series of such phrases: 'Not to be late on target, eh?'; 'Not to forget W/T silence, eh?'; and so on. This theory fits prettily with the common idiom in South African English 'Not so?', an abbreviation for 'Is it not so?', possibly influenced by the Afrikaans 'Ne?' and 'Nie waar nie?'.

Others ascribe the phrase to Americans. A small group pointed to Malta, and remembered their local staff saying such things as: *'Not to worry,* signor, the war is over.'

This last attribution matches interestingly an origin found in a Maltese analogy by the master of this sort of wild-goose chase, Eric Partridge. That choice and master wordsmith concluded in *A Dictionary of Catch Phrases,* published in 1977, that *not to worry* was current since the middle 1930s in the Services, and then suddenly in 1957-8 began to be generally and very widely used. He agrees with the suggestions that analogies from the Romance languages of a negative with an infinitive used as an imperative may have intervened. But he prefers his own theory that *not to worry* merely truncates 'you are *not to worry*'. Here the matter rests.

Another quite recent British English experiment in extension of *not* occurs in the phrase *not all that,* meaning 'not exceptionally so'. A tactless and ungallant example of this newish use is: 'Without her voice, Callas is *not all that* impressive an actress.' Once again analogies can be found on the Continent for the idiom, for example, the French *pas tellement. Not all that* is *not all that* new, though too recent to have been discussed in the *OED*. It has been in Northern dialect speech for many years, as, for example, in 'I'm *not all that* fussy', meaning 'I don't very much mind'. Perhaps the phrase is a natural extension of *that* for *so,* as in 'I was that ashamed I didn't know where to look', and the negative 'I'm not that poor I can't pay for myself'.

Both these extensions of *not* are new this century. Both are from British rather than American English. Both are rather odd. Both are colloquial. Both will undoubtedly be succeeded by equally illogical slang before long.

Don't blame Berlioz for this discordant note

For such a musical nation the British are oddly heavy-footed in their figurative use of musical terms. Our language is rich with metaphors drawn from the stage, from those competing chief protagonists who would have amazed Attic audiences accustomed to only one protagonist at a time, to role and scenario. But musical metaphors have never been so widely popular. We are prepared, if we are pretentious, to run up and down the whole gamut in scales and ranges other than musical ones. We speak of a person playing second fiddle, or blowing his own trumpet, or beating the drum for something.

Harmony, unison, and discord are used to describe conditions and activities other than musical. A *bandwagon* can be jumped, hopped, or climbed on by politicians and voters in a Gadarene stampede to be on the winning side, as well as by circus musicians carrying trombones and wearing funny hats. The earliest recorded example of a literal *bandwagon* occurs in P. T. Barnum's *Life* published in 1855: 'At Vicksburg we sold all our land conveyances excepting four horses and the bandwagon.' He was describing a difficult chapter in the life of his circus.

Humorous magazines started publishing cartoons depicting *bandwagons* carrying presidential hopefuls dressed as circus performers. Songs helped to popularize the figurative use of *bandwagons*. The Prohibitionists had a very successful temperance song called *The Prohibition Bandwagon* in 1900:

> 'And our friends who vote for gin,
> Will all scramble to jump in,
> When we get our big *bandwagon*,
> Some sweet day.'

Crescendo is almost always misused when out of a musical

E   129 context. It means a gradual process towards a climax or peak. The cliché 'to rise to a crescendo' is tautologous nonsense.

But much musical jargon is unexploited figuratively. It would seem strained to speak of a Prime Minister conducting his (or her) Cabinet as a *symphony*; in contrast with Sir Harold Wilson in the 1970 general election, who, on the advice of his principal private conductor, Lady Falkender, fought an unsuccessful presidential campaign as a virtuoso soloist in a violin concerto.

However, one technical term of music has suddenly become monotonously popularized in the cacophony of instant writing about politics, and that is the verb *to orchestrate*. Campaigns, opposition, speeches, infiltration, pressure groups, and all sorts of other unpleasant and decidedly unmusical activities are now said to be *orchestrated*, and often carefully *orchestrated*.

Orchestration or scoring is the art of setting out a composition for the instruments of an orchestra. The composer may score his music fully as he invents it, or first write it down in some kind of sketchy short score, or even in a pianoforte version. He is unlikely to use the last method unless he is so limited technically as to be constrained to compose at the piano. The art of *orchestration* has developed enormously since the early seventeenth century, but not necessarily improved. For good *orchestration* depends on the proper use of the resources available at any given time, not on the discovery of new ones, which may or may not have fortunate artistic results.

Methods of *orchestration* have also changed vastly. In the early seventeenth century Monteverdi roughed out his scores approximately, and they were played by such instruments as happened to be available. Bach chose a particular set of instruments to produce a particular tone-colour or timbre, and retained it throughout a whole work. Berlioz used a great range of instruments from one part to another, and may be said to have been the father of modern *orchestration*, since this is still the normal procedure.

From its musical sense of composing or arranging music for performance by an orchestra, *orchestrate* has come to be used figuratively. At first the metaphor stayed quite close to the orchestra, and meant to combine harmoniously like instruments in an orchestra, as in (1833) 'a symphony of accordant and *orchestrated* spirits'.

But recently it has come to be widely used to mean to organize, arrange, develop, or combine something or other so as to achieve a desired or the best result. Thus, a teller of tall tales should *orches-*

trate his facts, if he does not wish to expose himself as a liar. Conspirators, especially tightly knit groups of highly motivated men, *orchestrate* their activities and their stories. And separate lengths of time are *orchestrated* according to a novel's needs.

In January 1978 Margaret Thatcher spoke in Glasgow of 'carefully *orchestrated* euphoria' by the Government about the economy. In the same month the financial editor of *The Times* wrote of somebody putting forward his candidature 'to *orchestrate* the restructuring' of the British electronics industry. *Orchestrate* and *restructure* were both in the top ten O.K. words for 1978.

This new use is a welcome recruit to the moving toyshop of English metaphor, which is the principal way that the language grows and renews itself, with two qualifications. First, it is at present grossly over-used, and in danger of becoming a laughing-stock. Second, as a new metaphor its literal meaning is still close to the surface, and liable to be roused to rude life by incongruous contexts. When television showed the Queen and the Duke of Edinburgh on their silver jubilee tour of the Pacific leaving Fiji on the royal yacht, standing in the stern and dramatically floodlit, the commentator gave his opinion that the scene was beautifully *orchestrated*. We listened eagerly for the heavenly woodwinds and the surge of the Pacific percussion; or, at least, a harmonious blast from the *Britannia*'s horn. But music came there none. There was no sound at all, except the echo of an inappropriate metaphor falling flat.

Taking the Strain out of Strine

Ozzy: Hi there, pommie bastard. Why are you looking as pleased with yourself as a kookaburra that has swallowed a kangaroo?

Pommie: My aunt has given me *The Australian Oxford Dictionary.* Appropriately for the land of the marsupial, it is a pocket dictionary. So at last I shall be able to understand what you are saying, if you will speak a bit more slowly, old chap.

Ozzy: Even Blind Freddy can see what I mean without a dictionary, cobber. You are the one that talks funny, as if you have a tube of frozen Foster's stuck in your wind-pipe. But what do these drongos beyond the black stump at Oxford Uni-bloody-versity know about Oz?

Pommie: The dictionary was edited in Australia by the next best thing to a true-blue Australian, a New Zealander (it is an Oxford axiom that the best, indeed the only, lexicographers come from New Zealand). He was the late Professor Grahame Johnston of the Australian National University. His dictionary is the first serious attempt to provide an up-to-date guide to the English language as spoken in Australia and Earl's Court.

Ozzy: She'll be apples then. For a moment back there you gave me the dingbats, and I went crook on you, to think of high-falutin' pommie bastards high-hatting our beautiful Australian language. Does this bull artist really put in all our words?

Pommie: He appears to cover the Antipodes comprehensively.

There are the outback words from the backblocks to the back of beyond and Woop Woop, your expressive slang for a remote rural town or district. There is a big range of words connected with the bush. We have the bush-baptist, the bush carpenter, and the bush-lawyer, all of whom I wish to avoid, if possible. Nothing personal, you understand. There is your bonzer bushman with his bushcraft. There is the bushfire, of course, and the bush telegraph. You can get bush-sick, or just go bush. It is remarkable how much bush has come into English from your country.

Ozzy: Rattle your dags, man. I'll bet you a dollar you still don't know your jackaroo from a rouseabout.

Pommie: On the contrary, I am impressed by the conspicuously large group of words in Australian English that show how important sheep are, and have been in the country's economy. I like all your special wool-shed senses of words such as blades, blow, board, bin, class, clip and dagger. You have a talent for vivid slang from bare-bellies to kelpies, who apparently and delightfully derive their name from the original Scottish collie sheep-dog, called King's Kelpie, imported *circa* 1872.

Ozzy: My oath, pommie, you are learning. Beautiful Oz is a man's world, the land of the squatter, the runholder, and the grazier. The stockrider and the stock and station agent are characters in a story that goes back to Clancy of the Overflow. But can you understand the urban Strine that the ordinary man on the Canberra omnibus uses?

Pommie: I am becoming quite expert in all the Australian secular religions and preoccupations, from the Art Union to the trots, and from bikies to beer-ups. Bludger is a splendid word for a layabout. I think that Strine is particularly prolific and vigorous as a source of slang.

Ozzy: That's not slang, limey. That is the lively poetry of a language that has become stuck-up and effete in the old country.

Pommie: I agree that Strine is one of the fastest growing and most imaginative dialects of the great family of English-speakers. Strine originally meant the comic transliterations of uneducated Australian speech, for example, 'terror souse' to mean terrace house. It is now taken to mean the lingo of ockerism (aggressively Australian nationalism, speech, and behaviour, as evidenced, for instance, by Gough Whitlam).

Ozzy: Apart from our language, which I agree is more imaginative than yours, what do you make of the funny way that you pommies talk?

Pommie: *De pronuntiatione non disputandum.* The experts consider that there are fundamentally three styles of Australian pronunciation of English. They are not regional differences, because Australian English is remarkably uniform in different parts of the continent, but differences due to education, wealth, and other social factors.

Ozzy: You've made a real blue there, pongo, and caused me a lot of strife. What about the la-di-da way you talk? Do you know how a lecturer in English at your bloody Cambridge University defined received pronunciation? 'It is not the accent of a class but the accent of the class-conscious, the dialect of an effete social clique, half aware of its own etiolation, capitalizing linguistic affectations to convert them to caste-marks. Its taint of bogus superiority, its implicit snobbery make it resented. Its frequent slovenliness and smudge condemn it on purely auditory grounds.'

Pommie: I am not persuaded by that, old boy. I agree with the Oxford Professor who called received pronunciation 'the best kind of English, not only because it is spoken by those often very properly called the best people, but also because it has two great advantages that make it intrinsically superior to every other type of English speech—the extent to which it is current throughout the country and the marked distinctiveness and clarity of its sounds'.

Ozzy: There's nothing like you intellectuals for sticking their bibs in and going in boots and all, especially over something as trivial as pronunciation. But what do they say about pronunciation in Oz?

Pommie: The professionals of linguistics Down Under distinguish what they call General Australian (the variety spoken by the overwhelming majority), Cultivated Australian, and Broad Australian. They exist on a sliding scale in relation to received pronunciation, which is the educated speech of Southern England that you affect to find so funny. Cultivated Australian is closest to received pronunciation, the way I talk; then General Australian; with Broad Australian, the way you talk except when you forget to be aggressively ocker, most remote.

Ozzy: That sounds like sheer chunderous bastardry to me. Still, I'm not going to get off my bike. Let's not have a barney. She'll be right.

Enter Ozark, from Little Rock, Arkansas

Ozark: Say there, muscle-heads, dooze around and tell me by guess and by gosh what this advertisement by the United States Secretary for Health, Education, and Welfare* late in 1977 means: 'An extremely confidential personal assistant, responsible for managing, performing and supervising work related to the operation of the Secretary's kitchen and eating area.'

Ozzie: She'll be apples. What the stuck-up jackass wants is a good cook.

Pommie: Your Secretary evidently suffers from the tendency that Winston Churchill discerned in Ramsay MacDonald: 'the gift of compressing the largest number of words into the smallest amount of thought.' But tell me, Ozark, what is this new device of the U.S. Defense Department called 'a radiation enhancement weapon'?

Ozark: There's no tellin' what whomper-jawed words those fellers in Washington will come out with. I reckons as they're about two- or three-thirds drunk most of the time. But that thar weapon you mentioned is a purt-nigh tol'ble fancy name for the neutron bomb, that corn-shuckin' little crittur that kills people but leaves buildings intact.

Pommie: What a foul euphemism!

Enter Van der Merwe from Bloemfontein, wearing a blazer and waving a sjambok

Van der Merwe: Ag sis mon, this is lekker. Are you darem jolling,

---

* Joseph A. Californo Junior

or mos pronking? I can donder any man in the house.

Ozzy: Bring your dictionaries, pommie, and let us try to communicate with these ignorant bastards over the universal language of a few tubes of frozen Foster's.

35 / PERSONALITY

*Is there a person inside a
personality trying to get out?*

Who are these *personalities* who have recently come among us in
such excessive numbers? How do they differ from the rest of us
persons? They seem to have sprung fully armed with *personality*
from the television set. Indeed, to give their designation in full,
many of them are known as *television personalities.*

What they seem to be are persons whose faces are instantly
recognizable from exposure on television and in photographs in
newspapers, but who have no other obvious talents. Groucho Marx
appeared frequently on television, and his face is still instantly
recognizable. But he was described as a comedian or a genius, not
a *personality.*

Actors, actresses, dancers, singers, sportsmen, and professors
retain their professional descriptions and are not translated into
personalities, however often they appear on television, and however often persons in the street come up to them and say: 'I know
your face, don't I?' News-readers and persons like David Frost
and Hughie Green, who have become household faces merely by
frequent appearance on television, are such stuff as *personalities*
are made of. They have the sort of face that Madame Tussaud's
selects to represent in wax, to cater for the deep-rooted human
itch to rub shoulders with the famous, even at second-hand in wax.
This use of *personality* is somewhat older than television, though
television and the cinema nursed it to its full glory. Max Beerbohm
pioneered its use when he wrote of Bernard Shaw: 'As a teacher,
as a propagandist, Mr Shaw is no good at all, even in his own
generation. But as a *personality* he is immortal.'

In the six centuries that it has been part of the English language
personality has acquired a number of overlapping meanings, as is

E*   137 to be expected of such an old word. The oldest and primary meaning is the quality or state of being a person, and not an abstraction, thing, or lower being, as in (1692): 'We must be wary lest we ascribe any *personality* to this Nature or Chance.' If we are not wary in this matter, we shall be committing the *pathetic fallacy*, by crediting nature with human emotions. Burns was under the influence of the *pathetic fallacy* when he wrote:

> 'Ye banks and braes o' bonny Doon,
>> How can ye bloom sae fresh and fair?
> How can ye chant, ye little birds,
>> And I sae weary fu' o' care?'

The second main meaning is the assemblage of characteristics that makes a person what he is as distinct from other persons, by having a captivating, or, as it might be, a repellent *personality*. This sort of *personality* is a man's idiosyncrasy or make-up, the mixture of his elements, as in Brutus:

> 'His life was gentle, and the elements
> So mix'd in him that Nature might stand up
> And say to all the world, "This was a man!"'

Scott Fitzgerald used the word in this sense in *This Side of Paradise*: 'Monsignor was forty-two then, and bustling—a trifle too stout for symmetry, with hair the colour of spun gold, and a brilliant, enveloping *personality*. When he came into a room clad in his full purple regalia from thatch to toe, he resembled a Turner sunset.' Salinger used it in the derogatory sense in *The Catcher in the Rye*: 'He looked like the kind of a guy that wouldn't talk to you much unless he wanted something off you. He had a lousy *personality*.'

A third meaning is anything said of a person, especially in the way of disparagement or unfriendly reference. This sort of *personality* is usually in the plural, as in libellous *personalities*, from which, Good Lord, defend us. The word has acquired several other meanings and shades of connotation, some general, some specialized in the jargons of Law and Theology. In Law it means either personal belongings or the quality of concerning persons. In Theology it is applied to the distinct persons in the Godhead. One of these subsidiary meanings is a personal being, or, in short, a person. This *personality* combined with the idea of a striking *personality* that commands notice to make the modern film or television *personality*. He or she is a person of parts, importance, renown, or at any rate one who is often seen on television, as in 'a
138

gentle and lovable *personality*', or, more probably in this context, 'a loud and unlikable *personality*'.

A *personage* is also an exceptional sort of person, but for different reasons from the *personality*. A *personage* owes his importance to birth or high office. He is now more familiarly known as a VIP (very important person), a name invented for him during the last war by pilots and others to whose care such *personages* might be temporarily entrusted. A *personality* owes his fame to his talents in the world of entertainment, or at any rate to his frequent appearances on television. A *personality* receives far greater financial rewards than a *personage*.

The word has been further popularized by the *personality cult* practised by politicians as diverse, or perhaps as similar, as Kennedy and Khrushchev. This usage flatters a successful *personage* by promoting him to a *personality*, and transferring him from politics to show business. The Freudian jargon of *personality* tests and disorders has also influenced the word. The trouble about being a *personality* is that the career is often short though merry. And what can he do afterwards? One day he wakes up to the shock that the man in the street does not recognize his face any more. He has become a *non-personality*, and will have to try to grow up and become a person.

Persona is a technical term of literary criticism that is becoming fashionable outside the jargon. It is the Latin word for the mask worn by an actor in the classical theatre. Thence in Latin it came to mean a character in a play, and thence the role played by a person in life. In modern literary criticism *persona* is used to indicate the difference between the man who sits down to write and the 'author' as we realize him in and through the words on the page. This *persona,* or second self, of the author has to be distinguished from the narrator even in first-person narration. In Swift's *A Modest Proposal* (1729) the narrator in the first person proposes preventing the children of poor people from being a burden to their parents or the country of Ireland by using them as food for the rich. Swift's *persona* or second self, lurking sardonically behind the narrator, clearly recommends the opposite view: the improvement of conditions and provision of social remedies, not the breeding of children for food. This sort of *persona* serves a useful purpose in criticism. In the pretentious world outside, where it is used as a substitute for image or *personality,* it is *persona non grata.*

*An attachment à la Plato for a
bashful young potato or a not
too French French bean.*

Some odd and unsuitable freshmen have been enrolled in Plato's
Academy in the present academic year. An eminent diplomatic
commentator wrote the other day that the action taken by France
in response to atomic tests by South Africa would not be purely
platonic. And a leader in *The Times* volleyed and thundered with
more rhetoric than precision: 'The question facing the Carter
Administration now, therefore, is whether to let the difference between it and Mr Begin remain purely *platonic,* or to make clear to
Israel that it will not continue to finance and arm a Begin policy
it thinks will lead to war.' Aristocles son of Ariston, nicknamed
Plato, 'broad-shouldered', because of his prowess as a wrestler when
young, would be puzzled to know what he had to do with such
matters.

This recent new use of *platonic* is derived tortuously from the
Symposium, Plato's early and charming dialogue on the nature of
love, probably written in 384 B.C. Each of the guests at the famous
dinner party makes a speech in honour of love. Finally Socrates
sounds off, and takes the discussion to a higher plane. He says
that the need in the human being manifested on a lower plane by
the love of the sexes can also take an intellectual form: the desire
of the soul to create conceptions of wisdom and beauty, such as
poets and legislators produce. Man should proceed from the love
of a beautiful form (for Socrates likely to be that of a boy or young
man) to the perception and love of universal divine beauty. 'But
tell me,' he asked, 'What would happen if one of you had the luck
to look upon essential beauty entire, pure, and unalloyed: not
infected with the flesh and colours of humanity, and all the rest of

mortal trash?' This is an example of Plato's theory of ideal forms. Universal forms are, in his theory, absolutely distinct from things. In the same way our apprehension of them, which he calls knowledge, is absolutely distinct from opinion, which has to do with things. The easy, graceful, and humorous narrative of the *Symposium* shows how the love of a beautiful person can lead us to the love of wisdom and of the form of beauty itself.

Amor platonicus was introduced and used synonymously with *amor socraticus* by Ficinus (the Florentine, Marsilio Ficino, 1433-99), president of Cosimo de' Medici's *Accademia Platonica*, to denote the kind of interest in young men with which Socrates was credited in the last few pages of Plato's *Symposium*. As thus originally used, it had no reference to women. In English *platonic* love at first described both this sort of male homosexual love and, more often, the abstract love of beauty and wisdom commended in the *Symposium*. A letter of about 1645 defined the strange new passion: 'The Court affords little news at present, but that ther is a love, call'd *Platonick* Love, which much swayes there of late. It is a love that consists in contemplation and ideas of the mind, not in any carnall fruition.' Such *platonic* love was the longing of the soul for beauty; the inextinguishable desire that like feels for like, which the divinity within us feels for the divinity revealed to us in beauty. Some earthy cynics have taken the view that this kind of high *platonic* love is high *platonic* nonsense.

This lofty and philosophical sense of *platonic* love, from having originally meant a communion of two souls, and that in a rigidly dialectical sense, has gradually been degraded to the expression of maudlin sentiment between the sexes. This was the sort of relationship that John Bulwer had in mind when he wrote in *Anthropometamorphosis* (1650): 'The Mother-in-Law of Forestus, a fruitfull woman, would not match her daughters to *Platonique* men.'

Amor socraticus has now suffered another surprising vicissitude in its long, twisted journey from the *Symposium*. First it meant homosexual. Then it meant asexual, as in 'Till they dwindle into that stage of life, when, and when only, lovers become *Platonics* indeed'. It is evidently taken by some writers today to signify that one holds some opinion or feels some emotion without proposing to do anything practical about it. So we read of 'purely *platonic* protestations' and that 'if the majority has only a *platonic* belief in it, the law will break down'. Sir Herbert Beerbohm Tree said of an actress who was better as a lover than on the stage: 'She has

141

kissed her way into society. I don't like her. But don't misunderstand me: my dislike is purely *platonic*.' Gilbert Ryle, that witty categorist of categories, held that Plato was a very unreliable Platonist. He was too much of a philosopher to think that anything he had said was the last word. It was left to his disciples to identify his footmarks with his destination. Our recent taking of his name in vain has led us to some odd destinations.

37/ PRESENTS

Presenting a misleading appearance

Probation officers prepare documents called social inquiry reports on accused persons for the courts. These detail the childhood and career of the accused, and then go on to describe his or her personal appearance. At this point the report states: 'He *presents* as a bright (or dull, or downtrodden, or some other epithet) person.' This otiose new intransitive verb is now endemic in the probation service. It is an example of a common trend in the new Sociologese: the intransitive use of transitive or reflexive verbs. Other examples are 'he adjusts', 'he identifies', and 'he translates', used intransitively.

We profane outsiders, standing in awe at the threshold of the new temple of sociology listening to the mysteries, can see little need for this odd new use. 'He *presents* as a dull person' does not seem to say anything more than 'he looks dull'; 'he appears to be a dull person'; 'he *presents* himself as a dull person'; or 'he has a dull appearance'. No doubt we are wrong, and this new use conveys important new connotations and differentiations that cannot quite be conveyed by our existing vocabulary. But until the sociologists explain exactly what these new meanings are, we are bound to suspect them of being up to their old tricks of trying to hoodwink us with obscure and pretentious jargon.

The origin of this new intransitive use of *present* could be French, from the expression *présenter bien (ou mal)*, though why the Probation Service should look to French for its officialese is a puzzle. *Il se présente bien* (reflexive, not intransitive) means 'he is a man of good appearance'. In an English setting the intransitive verb is not presentable.

It is an old suspicion that sociology, being a new science that has not yet attracted as high academic esteem as it would like, tries to bluff disbelievers that it must be a grand new science, because it uses such grand new scientific language. In his interesting 1978 Reith Lectures Professor Albert Halsey, who is head of the department of social and administrative studies at Oxford University, took the courageous step of defining his brave new discipline. He said: 'Sociology is about social relations, the relations of individuals and groups in work and in play, war and peace, transient encounters and enduring bonds. Sociologists seek regularity and pattern in these relations. Hence they summarize them in abstractions as relations of production and reproduction, of kinship and affinity, of authority and freedom, power and advantage.' He suggested that two specific insights could be gained by adopting a sociological perspective: 'We shall discern the forces of continuity and change, and we shall arrive at a clearer view of what makes for consensus and conflict in our society.' Unfortunately few sociologists *present* as original in thought or as clear in expression as Professor Halsey. Social workers are as entitled as any other profession or group to their technical jargon, when they are writing for each other's eyes, but not when they come into court. Everybody does it to save time, as a form of shorthand.

Journalists use cable-ese or cablese, to save money. The master of this form of journalistic shorthand was John Bierman, who now works for Reuters and the BBC out of Cyprus. When in Central Africa he was famous for his ingenious service messages: CHECK-IMPOSSIBLE EVERYBODY OFFBUGGERED HILLWARDS (it is not possible either to confirm or deny the report you ask about because all the white bwanas have left the capital for the weekend to cool off in their private mountain retreats, and I have no means of getting in touch with them); and EXPRESSTORY PISTON EXGREATHEIGHT (the report that you tell me is being splashed in the *Daily Express* is vehemently and persuasively denied at the highest level). He used to sign such messages with the code name Alice Lane, which must have caused interest and speculation among the Post Office telegraphists. 'He *presents*' is shorter than some of the alternatives, and so saves time in writing reports. But does it say anything more than 'he looks', which is even shorter? Perhaps the advantage is that 'he *presents*' sounds more objective than 'he looks'.

The proper study of sociology is mankind and life in society. But if it uses man's ordinary language to describe its studies, it is afraid that they will be misunderstood; and despised as elementary.

144

However, it is not necessary to use complicated language to describe complicated thoughts. Ludwig Wittgenstein and Bertrand Russell managed to convey exceptionally complicated ideas in simple and lucid language. Sociologists have in fact made important new discoveries and opened new windows on the way we live in society. But their inveterate penchant for pretentious gobbledygook encourages the unkind suspicion that all that they are doing is 'obscurely systematizing the obvious', an activity also dear to journalists on occasions.

Professional euphemism as well as pretentiousness makes them say 'underprivileged', 'disadvantaged', or 'lower paid', when a plain man would say 'poor' or 'poorer', and convey the same meaning. This may be partly gentle tact. Some poor people may prefer to be described by the longer, obfuscatory words than the short, plain one. And for social workers 'underprivileged' and 'disadvantaged' include connotations other than the ancient problem of shortage of money: special problems of family, housing, schooling, and relationships with other people. The plain man would not be a social worker.

Sociologists are largely responsible for the plague of unnecessary 'situations' that rages and has spread to the media, as in 'the classroom situation', 'the industrial situation', and dozens of others every day. In that sort of prose any noun looks naked without its attendant situation. Why do sociologists say 'ongoing', when the rest of us manage perfectly well with 'continuing'? 'The case of' is usually superfluous, and 'the existence of' is invariably superfluous. 'To look at' something is lazy, ill-defined, and vague, when we could examine, re-examine, appraise, reappraise, or simply think about it.

It would be possible to construct a table for producing a completely meaningless general-purpose memorandum in the jargon of sociology, as debased by journalists and other popularizers. The table would consist of lists of such popular terms as:

Ad hoc	Meaningful
Adumbration	Multidisciplinary
At this moment in time	Ongoing
Conceptualize	Real-time
Environmental	Throughput
Lateral	Valid
Low-profile	Viable

145

The rules of the game are as follows:

1. Perm the terms so that the memorandum is equally (in)appropriate in all contexts.
2. The memorandum must appear to have a meaning.
3. The words linking the jargon must be chosen so as to leave the greatest possible doubt whether they are adverbs, prepositions, verbs, or nouns, so that the entire assembly is as fluid a piece of abstract art as possible.

For example, the Open University on writing essays: 'Your TMA is a function of the continuous assessment element in our learning system.' A TMA, by the way, is OU-Speak for an essay. Obfuscationwise the Open University is in a multidisciplinary and ongoing linguistic doghouse situation.

*The perils of pristine,
which does not mean Pearl White*

In a recent novel about life on a thinly disguised Sunday newspaper, the heroine, who is as careless with the English language as she is reckless with her body, at one point puts on a *pristine* cream blouse. This makes a change from her usual practice of whipping off her clothes at the slightest intimation of interest by a member of the opposite, or, for that matter, the same sex. Fortunately no dog plays a major part in the rubbish.

When putting on her *pristine* blouse the awful columnist heroine is in even worse company than she usually keeps, in that she appears to believe that *pristine* means new, fresh, and as clean as a new pin. It actually means original or antique: almost the opposite of a new pin. If we must give the nymphomaniac fictional heroine the benefit of the doubt, and she does not deserve it, we must suppose her to mean that her blouse is as good as new, showing no signs of wear since she bought it from an advertisement in one of the colour magazines eight years ago. Such thrift is out of character.

The delusion that *pristine* is an impressive synonym for new has become so prevalent among the fashionable ignorant that the unhappy word is being stood on its head. By consensus of error it will soon come to mean the opposite of its original and etymologically correct meaning. One of the charms of English is that it is always moving with the times faster than other languages. But the recent sudden movement of *pristine* is unnecessary, and wastes a good word.

It comes from the Latin *pristinus*, which means belonging to olden times, antique, ancient; former or previous; that has already existed for some time. *Pristina nox* means the night before. In

147

Latin *tunica pristina* (the pristine cream blouse) would mean the old blouse that she had had for some time. Primitive, primeval, and pri(s)mus share the same stem. In English the word *pristine* means of or pertaining to the earliest period or state; original, former; primitive, primeval, ancient. The citations in the *Oxford English Dictionary* clearly illustrate its use in these senses from the sixteenth century onwards.

The earliest recorded example comes from a letter of Anne Boleyn in 1534, when she wrote of restoring someone to his *pristine* freedom. In subsequent centuries it made sense to talk of reducing the said parties to their *pristine* amity. An expedition set out for the recovery of their *pristine* possession. Matthew Prior wrote:

> 'Hence then, close Ambush and perfidious War,
> Down to your *pristin* Seats of Night repair.'

Somebody was said to have spoken and prophesied like a sage of some *pristine* era. Something was restored to its *pristine* purity. Translators were commended for having happily preserved for us the *pristine* simplicity of our Saxon English. Empedocles is said to have believed in a *pristine* state of happiness: a belief with which many philosophers have consoled themselves for the unsatisfactory state of affairs they found in their contemporary world.

That last quotation gives a clue to the reason why *pristine* has turned topsy-turvy. Like Empedocles, we are often dissatisfied with our human condition, and look back wistfully to what we suppose was a primitive or *pristine* golden age. So did the Romans look back in nostalgia to *Saturnia regna,* when the world was young, fruit grew on every tree without cultivation, and sheep came with their fleeces already dyed; so did other Greeks fed up with contemporary politics in addition to Empedocles. In fact in Empedocles's world-cycle of generation and decay, the golden age is in the future as well as in the past; so perhaps for him *pristine* could as well mean new as old. The past often seems rosier than the nasty present, though for *pristine* contemporaries, no doubt, it was quite as solitary, poor, nasty, brutish, and short as we find life in our melancholy moods today.

From its connotations of the primitive, primeval world, it was a short step for *pristine* to come to mean uncorrupted by civilization or the world. That which is in its original state cannot have been corrupted or adulterated, because it has not had time to be. It made sense to speak of *pristine* innocence or freshness. And the innocence and the freshness rubbed off on the old adjective, *pristine,* for those

148

who were not sure what it meant, and could not be bothered to look it up in a dictionary.

A theological explanation of how *pristine* came to be both old and new is to say that what is *pristine* is close to its source, like spring water, pure, fresh, and new. Passing time, through which all things become old, eliminates the *pristine*, which, however, may be renewed from moment to moment in the now; 'for the source does not lie in passing time, but at the point of intersection of time and the timeless.'

The antiquarian book trade still uses *pristine* carefully in its original and *pristine* sense, to describe an early book in good condition, in the original boards, and uncut.

In the less careful world outside bookshops it has come to be supposed that *pristine* itself means something like free from drabness, soil, or decay; fresh, clean, and unsophisticated, as we sentimentally and erroneously imagine the golden ages of antiquity to have been. So a holiday advertisement describes snow that has just fallen as '*pristine* powder'. Good writers and talkers do not use the word in this new sense. The hack who wrote of 'a *pristine* and fabulously wealthy residential area' was not a good writer; and she got fabulously wrong too.

39/ QUANTUM

*Leaping into physics and coming
out with a quantum jump*

To read the newspapers these days you would suppose that we poor hacks have taken up theoretical physics, a rigorous subject ill-suited to our flibbertigibbet minds. *Quantum jump* is becoming a modish journalistic phrase. We use it to mean a sudden spectacular advance; a major break-through (a vogue word itself from Pentagonese or MoDSpeak); an unusually large and sudden increase in a quantity that normally varies slowly. It is replacing that most hackneyed and intrusive of quotations, sea change from *The Tempest*.

When Opec (the Organization of Petroleum Exporting Countries) unilaterally and dramatically increased the price of oil in 1970, a thousand typewriters leaped from their cases to describe its action as a *quantum* leap in prices.

The Times used it twice on the same day in 1977 to describe the sudden steep rise in Soviet air power and an expected unprecedented increase in rail speed records. Here is a good example of the new figurative use from *New Scientist*, which ought to know better: 'The ability of marine technology to take *quantum* leaps in innovation means that a laissez-faire approach to the ocean mineral resources can no longer be tolerated.'

Our use of *quantum jump* as a popularized technicality is enough to send Planck and Einstein into a molecular spin in their graves. As often happens when journalists filch the technical jargon of a difficult subject, we have got hold of the wrong end of the quark. A *quantum jump* in theoretical physics means almost the exact opposite of its popular use in journalism. Our sub-editors should make us walk the Planck when we misuse the metaphor.

In 1901 Max Planck, the German physicist, introduced the idea
150

that electromagnetic radiation could be emitted or absorbed only in minute discrete *quanta*. A *quantum* is one of the very small increments or parcels into which many forms of energy are subdivided. A *quantum jump* is an abrupt transition (as of an electron, an atom, or a molecule) from one discrete energy state to another, with absorption or emission of a *quantum*.

Planck demonstrated that the Latin proverb, *Natura non facit saltus*, Nature does not make jumps, was wrong. He showed that radiation by a body is an interrupted process, each radiator emitting energy in equal amounts termed *quanta*, the value of which depends on a universal constant and the frequency of the vibrations of the radiators. Planck's constant (generally written h) relates the mechanical properties of matter to its wave properties. The energy of a particle determines its frequency according to the equation: frequency = energy divided by h. Those who know about such things confidently assert that $h = 6.6256$ multiplied by 10^{-34} Newton metre seconds or Joule seconds.

Those whose heads are made to ache by such assertions can simply regard a *quantum* as a discrete packet of energy, a minimum that is indivisible. Accordingly, in its scientific meaning, a *quantum jump* describes a transition between states of a physical system that can exist only in a finite number of states, the jumps being tiny, and the system not being allowed to vary between jumps.

As *quantum* mechanics was developed in the 1920s, it revealed an idea of movement startlingly different from that in classic physics. In the classic, Newtonian world, one state of affairs could turn into another by a smooth, continuous process. Any position along a continuum was theoretically possible. *Quantum* or wave mechanics, based on the wave-particle duality of matter and radiation, was discovered to describe systems so small that Newtonian mechanics broke down. This discovery that in the minute roots of Nature some things can only happen in leaps and bounds was one of the greatest intellectual triumphs of this century.

A more accurate use of the metaphor, therefore, would be to describe every change in Soviet air power of one single aircraft, and every increase in rail speed records by a single mile an hour as a *quantum jump*.

What we journalists evidently need is a mathematical term to describe a sudden sharp increase. We could try 'of a new order of magnitude'. Exponential growth can be very fast, but it is a continuous process. Its inverse is the logarithmic function. Pity

151

the poor logarithm; it creeps up more slowly than anything else around—excepting the logarithm of the logarithm. We could try 'hyperbolically', which has the advantage that, in addition to its mathematical meaning, it gives warning of the extravagant exaggeration. Or we could delve further into mathematics, and discover catastrophe theory, which explicitly analyses sudden change. There we shall find the terms 'fast action' of Professor Erik Zeeman, and 'catastrophe' of Professor R. Thom used to describe this phenomenon. Catastrophe appears to be an excellent term for changes in Soviet air power and rail speeds. 'Discontinuous' is a mathematical term that could be used to describe a sudden, sharp increase. But then 'sudden' and 'sharp', though less showy, are useful words for the purpose.

We are beguiled by the kangaroo connotations of the *quantum jump*, and the delusion that *quantum* means a very big rather than a very small quantity. Perhaps we could extend our figurative use of physics. The report of a soccer match in a pretentious newspaper might then read:

'Although, under its new manager, the selection of the England team was Heisenbergian, nevertheless its style of play remained decidedly Laplacean. In spite of the well-known Brownian motion of the Liverpool players, their efforts culminated, alas, in the familiar Keplerian cross to the far post, with nobody there to make a *quantum jump* to meet it. On the other hand, the passing of the opposition exemplified an Aristotelian tendency to stick to earth. If the shooting of our front runners was, to say the least, failed Rutherford, the positioning of the central defenders can only be described as pre-Copernican. England's overall performance has to be judged, of course, in Einsteinian perspective. Better, perhaps, failure and the Ptolemaic after-match comments of the new manager than success and the obscure Pythagoreanisms of his predecessor.'

40/ QUARK

For the quark was a boffin, you see

Other men's technical jargon is none of our business. We may shake our heads sadly when the BBC and other hi-fi enthusiasts decide to call their latest expensive gadget quadraphony or quadraphonics, each of which is a centaur word, having a Latin head and a Greek tail. The BBC makes them more absurd by pronouncing them quadrOphony and QuadrOphonics. The thoroughbred word would be either tessaraphonics in Greek, or quadrivocals in Latin, neither of which is a horse one would put one's shirt on. Nevertheless, the world is full of herds of centaur words, from bicycle to television. Televiewer seems to be giving way to the thoroughbred, viewer. In due course television itself may lose its incongruous horse's tail, and become the plain telly. It is tidier and more elegant to form a new word from one language at a time. But it would be unreasonable and impertinent to demand that neologism should be conducted so as to avoid making purists wince. And who would listen to us? The English language can no longer be run (if indeed it ever has been) so as to avoid giving offence to classical scholars. Pioneers of new scientific frontiers must blaze the trail with the new words that suit them.

However, some technical terms invented for a jargon are so brilliant that they show what can be done by scientists with a little imagination. Let us now praise famous coiners of words, and the happy nomenclators that begat them. Despite extensive searches by nuclear physicists for the past decade, no *quarks* have yet been observed. But that, if anything, improves the appropriate beauty of the name of the elusive little creatures.

Early in this century scientists were beginning to understand how the atom is made up of electrons surrounding a central nucleus. The next step was the investigation of the nucleus itself, and the realization that it too is made up of still smaller particles, called neutrons and protons. In the 1960s, physicists started to look into the structure of these neutrons and protons too. It was suggested that the understanding of these nuclear particles would be easier if they in turn were deemed to be made up of sub-particles.

In 1964 Professor Murray Gell-Mann, a brilliant physicist at the California Institute of Technology, suggested using *quark* for his theory that three basic states of matter make up, in different combinations, all the hundred-plus particles found so far in the heart of the atom. To Professor Gell-Mann *quarks* are simply mathematical symbols useful in explaining the unstable, strange new world of subatomic particles that mock all attempts at understanding. A *quark* is one of three different hypothetical particles that might be the structural units from which many of the elementary particles are constructed. *Quarks* have the unusual property that their electric charges are multiples of one-third of the charge of the electron. It is not essential that *quarks* actually exist. Indeed, there is still no evidence that they do, though scientists continue to dream up experiments to hunt down the bark of the *quark*.

Gell-Mann took the admirably expressive name from the opening words of chapter four, book two of James Joyce's *Finnegans Wake:*

'Three *quarks* for Muster Mark!
Sure he hasn't got much of a bark
And sure any he has it's all beside the mark.'

Joyce slyly, wryly, and aptly observed that *quarks* are damnably elusive. He used the word to describe the mocking call of the seagulls to King Mark in the Arthurian legend, as he lies helpless, dreaming of his bride Iseult in the arms of Tristan.

Quark is also, enchantingly, the local pet name for a rare bird found only in the Falkland Islands. Its scientific name is *Nycticorax Cyanocephalus Falklandicus.* It is said to be a bird of great beauty, like a heron in appearance, with silky green plumage and a single multicoloured feather that streams out behind the head in flight. It is familiarly called *quark* by the Falkland Islanders because of the strangely beautiful call it makes when disturbed.

Finally to *quark* is an obsolete, onomatopoeic word meaning to croak, as in (1860) 'the gurgling and *quarking* of spring frogs in a pond', and (1893) 'rooks cawing and *quarking*'.

The latest development in the hunting of the *quark* is the theory that certain *quarks* carry a special property known as 'charm'. Experiments seem to confirm the existence of charmed *quarks,* but

154

also indicate that there may be two additional *quarks*. An ephemeral particle ten times heavier than the proton and neutron of the atomic nucleus, heaviest of the stable particles, suggests the existence of six rather than four *quarks* as basic building blocks of matter. These two additional *quarks* are now being referred to as *'top quark'* and *'bottom quark'*, or, by the jolly nuclear physicists with their excellent tradition for whimsical names, as 'truth' and 'beauty'. The newly reported superheavy particle would imply the existence of 'beauty', alias the *bottom quark*. The validity of this interpretation would be strengthened by further experiments, including those indicating that 'truth' also exists.

It does not matter whether the scientists ever catch a *quark*. In such a majestic chase true sportsmen will be on the side of the *quark*, as they are of the fox. But the physicists are to be congratulated and thanked for their delightful piece of jargon.

Boffin is another charming piece of jargon invented mysteriously during the war. Originally it meant an 'elderly' naval officer, that is, one aged thirty-two or more. There was even a song about them:

> 'He glares at us hard and scowls,
> For we're the Flotilla *Boffins*.'

Then it came to mean a person engaged in 'back-room' scientific or technical research. The name seems to have been first applied by members of the Royal Air Force to scientists working on radar.

Numerous conjectures have been made about the origin of the word, but all lack foundation. It may have had something to do with an obsolete type of aircraft called the Baffin, and something to do with the bird called the puffin. Eric Partridge takes a glance at 'baffle' (the bafflings = the baffling fellows = those who baffle the enemy), and perhaps at 'The Boffin Books', a delightful series for children.

The name probably had nothing to do with that first literary back-room boy, the claustrophiliac Colonel Boffin, and nothing to do either with Nicodemus or 'Noddy' Boffin, the Golden Dustman in Dickens's *Our Mutual Friend*. That Boffin was the former confidential servant and foreman to John Harmon's father, who left him a fortune on his death. He was: 'A broad, round-shouldered, one-sided old fellow in mourning, coming comically ambling towards the corner, dressed in a pea overcoat, and carrying a large stick. He wore thick shoes, and thick leather gaiters, and thick gloves like a hedger's. Both as to his dress and to himself, he was of an overlapping rhinoceros build, with folds in his cheeks, and his forehead, and his eyelids, and his lips, and his ears; but with bright, eager, childishly-inquiring grey eyes, under his ragged eyebrows, and broad-brimmed hat. A very odd-looking old fellow altogether.'

Unfortunately, though engaging and exhibiting many characteristics of the *boffin*, he does not seem to have been the ancestor of the back-room boys from Farnborough. The fanciful name resonates more with echoes of Lewis Carroll than of Dickens. We shall have to leave the etymology in the circular condition that *boffins* are called *boffins* because they behave like *boffins* and indulge in *boffinry*. Whatever its derivation, *boffin*, like *quark*, is a fine recruit to the English language. If all jargons were so imaginative and inventive, the language would be an even more beautiful and varied jungle.

It is as cheap sitting as standing

According to Franz Kafka, only our concept of time makes it possible for us to speak of the Day of Judgment by that name. In reality it is a summary court in perpetual *session*. If so, it might spare a moment from its awful labours to make sure that it is sitting comfortably in time. *Session* is being widely adopted, especially by sporting journalists and commentators, as if it meant a length of time. Switch on the television set any Saturday afternoon, if you can bear it, and you will hear such grotesque misnomers as *sessions* of cricket, of football, of boxing, and of the more arcane sports for which the broadcasting authorities have so great a predilection. Sporting writers are eager to persuade the rest of us to take the playful activities from which they earn their livings as seriously as they do, and think to do so by borrowing the serious language of the law courts and Parliament. Conversely, politicians and other public men lighten and popularize their serious discourse by adopting sporting terms as metaphors. It was a brilliant flash of rhetorical lightning for Montgomery to tell the Eighth Army that they were going to hit Rommel for six right out of Africa. It made the blood, toil, tears, sweat, and sand that lay ahead sound a game of cricket.

Session comes by way of French from the Latin *sedere*, to sit, and clearly shows its sedentary Latin connexion. The enchanting old word a *sederunt* (they sat), meaning a sitting of a deliberative or judicial body, now chiefly of an ecclesiastical assembly, has the same root. Old-fashioned gentlemen in Scotland use *sederunt* jocularly to mean an informal chat, generally, as such matters are arranged in Scotland, over a bottle.

Accordingly, *session* means primarily the action or an act of sitting; the state or posture of being seated; the occupation of a seat

157

in an assembly or the like. An early book of anatomy called *The
Body of Man* (1615) caught its fundamental meaning well, when
it declared that on the foreside (by which it meant the backside)
the body 'is gibbous, and that is profitable for *session*'. It is therefore an appropriate word to use of bishops or kings in *session* in
council; of Caesar in the Senate; of Christ seated at the right hand
of God; of Members of Parliament and other dignitaries in *session*
(in British parliamentary use a *session* is the period between the
opening of Parliament, usually in the autumn, and its prorogation,
usually in the following autumn); of judges at great or petty
sessions; of Lords President, and councillors, and bridge-players
and all persons in such sedentary occupations.

> 'Then of their *session* ended they bid cry
> With trumpet's regal sound the great result.'

Some universities in Scotland and the United States describe a
term as a *session*, on the reasonable ground that they are seats of
learning.

The word is wildly inappropriate to describe such vigorous and
generally standing activities as cricket (unless you take the arrogant
spectator's view that all other men's catches are sitters); as boxing
(though the phrase conjures up a delightful vision of Muhammad
Ali bounding around the ring on his bottom: bounce like a flea,
sting like a bumble-bee); or as football (after a back pass the striker
missed a sitter?). According to the newspapers the Stock Exchange
now has daily *sessions*. The expression suggests the engaging idea
of all those stockbrokers in pin-striped suits staging a sit-in on the
floor of the House. But actually they do not sit; they scurry around
on their feet, as busily as ants. The most famous ice rink in London
uses unconscious irony when it chooses the perfect word to advertise its 'beginners' *sessions* daily'.

A man would be batting on a sticky wicket and queering his own
pitch if he insisted that *session* could never be used except for
sitting. Applied generally, such a crass rule would prohibit all
metaphor, which is the principal flower-bed for new and vivid
language. Sitting was not the uppermost image in Shakespeare's
mind, although the law courts were there, when he began one of
his most haunting sonnets:

> 'When to the *sessions* of sweet silent thoughts
> I summon up remembrance of things past.'

Obsession originally meant the action of sitting down before a
fortress to besiege it. Thence by metaphor it came to be used of an
158

evil spirit or incubus besetting somebody; and thence came the transferred modern use in Freudian English of a fixed idea that persistently besieges somebody's mind. Very many of our words are used metaphorically in this way. Some have been so used for so long that the metaphor is stone-dead, as, for example, in *examine,* which originally and literally meant to weigh or assay from the Latin *examen,* the tongue of a balance. Not even a faint echo of weighing-scales comes to mind any longer when we *examine* something.

Hat-trick is another term that is being adopted metaphorically and loosely by sporting writers, though its adoption is not objectionable or ludicrous. A *hat-trick* originally meant a piece of legerdemain (or perhaps, strictly, legerdetête) practised by a conjuror. In the nineteenth century there was a common parliamentary practice called the *hat-trick,* in which a Member of Parliament reserved his seat in the House of Commons by placing his hat on it. Then it came into cricket jargon to mean the feat of a bowler who takes three wickets with successive balls. This achievement was considered to entitle the bowler to be presented by his club with a new hat or some equivalent. Its first recorded use, from Lillywhite's *Cricketers' Companion* of 1877, records what was evidently a *top hat trick*: 'having on one occasion taken six wickets in seven balls, thus performing the *hat-trick* successfully'.

The phrase is being loosely adapted to describe a threefold feat in other sports or activities. Thus Red Rum was said to have completed a *hat-trick,* erroneously, because his victories in the Grand National were not consecutive. Political parties are said, more accurately, to have recorded a *hat-trick* of victories. British aircraft manufacturers in 1931 hoped that an official attempt would be made on the world height record, and the *hat-trick* accomplished by the annexation of all three of the records that really mattered in aviation. And footballers are often said to have scored *hat-tricks,* when strictly they have not: all they have done is to score three goals, not consecutive goals, in an afternoon. This extension of the term vexes only pedants. The fashionable abuse of *session* is more serious, because it is spoiling a useful word.

O sancta simplicitas: making a virtue of simplicity

Truth is seldom pure, rarely simple, and never *simplistic*. This does not prevent truth, on its occasional and timid appearances in public, from being so described. *Simplistic* has recently become a very fashionable depreciatory word in the war of ideas, used to put down arguments with which the speaker does not agree.

What seems to have happened is that in our increasingly complicated society simplicity has been undergoing a rapid process of betterment. We look back wistfully to the days when we simple souls had not yet been introduced to our subconsciousnesses and the other complicating facts of modern life. Accordingly simplicity has become not a mere quality, but a virtue; and its formerly unfavourable senses of 'mean', 'credulous', and 'silly' have receded. A new word has therefore been introduced, partly to express these unfavourable senses of 'simple'.

Historically, *simplistic* used to mean 'of or pertaining to simples or a simplicist' (a person who collects or is skilled in medicinal herbs or simples). John Donne wrote in an essay: 'As Simplicists which know the venom and peccant quality of every herbe but cannot fit them to Medicin.' The pun, confounding a herbalist with Simple Simon, was always recognized, for example in the old proverb: 'Go to Battersea to be cut for the simples.' Francis Grose in *A Classical Dictionary of the Vulgar Tongue* published in 1785 explains: 'Battersea is a place famous for its garden grounds, some of which were formerly appropriated to the growing of simples for apothecaries, who at a certain season used to go down to select their stock for the ensuing year, at which time the gardners were said to cut their simples; whence it became a popular joke to advise young people to go to Battersea, at that time, to have their simples cut, or to be cut for the simples.'

This use is now both obsolete and otiose. Herbalism is no longer an important sprig of science. And modern chemical analysis has shown that simple is an inappropriate name for a medicinal herb, whose combination of compounds is likely to be far more complex than any medicine in a modern pharmacopoeia. Our ancestors called such a herb a simple because it was a single uncompounded and unmixed medicament or ingredient.

Simplistic in its modern sense was introduced into English directly from the French. Originally, like many such variant introductions, it was a technical term of the jargon of literary criticism: 'Other writers have to affect what to Wordsworth is natural; so they have what Arnold calls *simplism,* he simplicity.' Wordsworth's word was simpler and better than Arnold's.

Simplicity or over-simplification is better for most purposes than simplism, which has not established itself outside the muddy and pretentious waters of Sociologese. But there is evidently a need for its adjective *simplistic* in ordinary speech to ridicule arguments, ideas, or attitudes of extreme or affected simplicity. It describes a tendency to concentrate on a single aspect (for example, of a problem) to the exclusion of all complicating factors. The division of mankind exclusively into workers and capitalists is a *simplistic* and fallacious classification. The facts of nature and of life are more likely to be complex than simple. The universe is not only more complex than we know, but very probably more complex than we can know. *Simplistic* theories are generally one-sided and partial, and consequently not theories at all, but hypotheses, or perhaps mere expressions of opinion. Most generalizations are *simplistic,* including this one.

It was a witty definition to say that *simplistic* simply means the inability to distinguish between simple and *simplistic.* But the word is now so overused that it is in danger of becoming a fashionable parrot cry and thence a laughing-stock. Those who value simplicity as a virtue will find that in most contexts simple or over-simplified will do the job better than *simplistic.*

43/ WALKABOUT

Is it progress to go on royal walkabout?

It would be churlish and out of tune with the traditional British respect for their monarchy to say that the Queen had gone loco and abo, and had run away from her duty to get away from it all. Yet that, of course, is what we are saying every time we describe her, as we seem to be doing whenever she visits anywhere these days, as *going walkabout*, or, less idiomatically, *doing a walkabout*. Since the Queen's visit to Australia in 1969 *walkabout* has been widely adopted as a technical term of the royal family business, to mean an informal stroll by a public figure to meet the people whom chance or a carefully-briefed equerry throws in her way.

Royals strolled informally among their subjects long before the term was introduced. There was nothing remote or inaccessible about Charles II. He received ambassadors amid the unchecked throng of his subjects, and pulled off his hat to the meanest as he took his walk in the park or galleries. Charles found it so hard to say 'no' to the petitioners who dogged and hounded his strolls in St James's Park that he cultivated a very fast gait, scattering non-committal 'God bless you's on either side as profusely as he scattered bread to the ducks. William IV enjoyed mixing with the crowds in London and Brighton, bowing to those who caught his eye, and doing what Lyndon Johnson used to describe as pressing the flesh (shaking hands). A few days after his accession he decided to take a walk down St James's Street, unattended by any of his courtiers. He was quickly recognized, hustled, and cheered, and a patriotic prostitute saluted her new Sovereign with a kiss. When he was rescued, he said: 'Oh, never mind all this: when I have walked about a few times they will get used to it.' His successors to the British Throne would not agree with his judgment that familiarity decreases the public appetite for ogling royalty.

162

The Queen herself, when she visited the United States as Princess Elizabeth in 1951, was taken by Harry Truman on what would today be called a *walkabout* through New York.

Walkabout is a term of pidgin English. Pidgin English means 'Business English', and was the name given by the Chinese to the Anglo-Chinese lingua franca. They pronounced business 'pidgin', and we have confused the meaningless 'pidgin' with the significant pigeon. Hence comes the curious expression 'That's not my pigeon.' From Anglo-Chinese pidgin has been extended to mean any combination and distortion of two languages as a means of communication. *Walkabout* comes from the vivid pidgin composed of Australian English and Australian Aboriginal languages. An expert suggests that the correct way to address the Queen in pidgin, in the unlikely event of finding her going real *walkabout*, would be something like: 'Feller find it hard going blackfeller fashion. Which-way you been gitchim dat big bugger? All same blackfeller long o' bush.'

The same pidgin gives us a delightful version of Christianity:

> *The god-men say when die go sky*
> > *Through Pearly Gates where river flow,*
> *The god-men say when die we fly*
> > *Just like eagle-hawk and crow—*
> *Might-be, might-be; but I don't know.*

When the Queen goes *walkabout* her object is to meet and be seen by as many people as possible. When an Australian Aborigine goes *walkabout* he goes off into the outback to wander in the bush for a while, to get away from his regular work and the pressures of the twentieth century that are turning Australia into a suburb masquerading as a continent. *Walkabout* is usually a lonely, sometimes a demented, and always a dangerous activity, since it is hard to survive on one's own in the desert. It is expressive pidgin for the urge felt by the Aboriginal station hand to discard the trappings of white 'civilization', and go native, until such time as he feels sufficiently spiritually refreshed to return to his job.

Instances have been reported of whole tribes going *walkabout*, to withdraw from the civilization that has pauperized them, and find some magico-religious escape in the *Karangara* or Kimberleys, and a lost world where the *Dreaming* has not been polluted by the white man, who does not remember to tread softly because he treads on other men's dreams. But *walkabout* is generally done by a solitary man who wants to be on his own away from crowds.

163

For the Queen to go *walkabout* she would need to tell the crowds to go to hell, put on a loin cloth, and beat it into the interior. It is an engaging trick of the restless and universal ocean of the English language that the word has now been adopted to describe a ceremonial passage by a royal personage through vast, staring, pressing crowds.

The alternative colloquial phrase, *walkaround*, has been pre-empted as a technical term of jazz. According to *Funk and Wagnalls* it means a dancing performance by Negroes during which the dancer describes a large circle. 'Dixie' was composed in 1859 by Dan D. Emmett as a *walkaround* for Bryant's Minstrels. So it is almost as inappropriate a word to describe the Queen meeting her people as *walkabout*. *Walk-on* is no good, because it has been adopted to describe an air-service or aeroplane, for which one does not have to buy a ticket in advance and which is sometimes cheaper than the regular air-service. The appropriate words from medieval royal terminology are 'progress' and 'chevachee' (in its origins a doublet of cavalcade), but it is difficult to imagine either of these catching on again. For the Queen to perambulate among her people might conjure up visions of her pushing a baby carriage.

What's what between who and whom

Now that English has become largely an uninflected language, it is not surprising that we occasionally get ourselves into a muddle with our few case-forms that survive, and say things like 'It's me' or 'Between you and I'. Orson Welles is used to advertise in large headlines: 'At last—a sherry for we Amontillado connoisseurs.' Somebody, striving for correctitude, recently published the sentence: 'I refer to he who is known as Shakespeare.' The *Washington Star* ran a long and heated correspondence in 1977 to try to establish whether *whoever* or *whomever* was right in the phrase: 'To make that speech absolutely clear and lucid to *whomever* is listening.' It read like Hansard of a parliament of owls: 'Who-whom, who-whom.'

The late Cardinal Heenan was a stickler for correct grammar. He was succeeded in 1976 as Archbishop of Westminster by Cardinal Hume. The Roman Catholic grammarian's joke at the time was that when Cardinal Heenan ascended to Heaven, God's first question to him was: 'Who would you like as your successor?' 'Whom' corrected the Cardinal.

Sometimes our errors in case-forms are simple confusion. Sometimes they are deliberate, splendid defiance of grammar, in order not to sound pedantic or prissy. A newspaper editor recently wrote to *UK Press Gazette* ('for journalists and all who work with them') drawing attention to an example of *who* used incorrectly: Westminster Press had asked in an advertisement: 'Who do they guard?' *UK Press Gazette* remarked in an editorial footnote: 'There is an alternative view that pedantry rates higher than colloquialism on the editorial sin-meter.'

Placards advertising evening newspapers regularly trail observations by the Prince of Wales with the words 'Marriage and Me' in big, black type. Sub-editors on evening newspapers have a taste for alliteration. And the way that the Prince's mother starts her speeches, 'My husband and I', is felt to be quaintly correct as in an elocution class, as well as charmingly whatever adjective is the wifely feminine of uxorious. The adjective you are looking for is the extremely rare word 'maritorious'.

In colloquial English, when the interrogative pronoun comes first and the verb or preposition governing it comes last, it is common to say *who* instead of *whom*; as in, 'Who did you hear that from?', and, 'Who did you see there?'. Thus Bamber Gascoigne in the television quiz programme 'University Challenge' asks, 'Who do I mean when I refer to the red-headed sage of Cowdenbeath?'; and would sound pompous if he said *whom*. Nevertheless, the use is strictly ungrammatical, and is so described by grammars and dictionaries. It looks bad in formal writing.

Its badness was widely on view in 1977 in a series of advertisements published by the Advertising Standards Authority, the British advertising industry's home-bred watchdog that tries to enforce a voluntary code of practice on its masters. These started with a photograph of some personality (an interesting new use), and a headline that ran: 'Dear Marge,' (or, as it might be, Fred) 'If you saw an advertisement that offended you, *who* would you write to?'

Leon Pilpel, the sapient and fastidious chief sub-editor of *The Times*, saw this advertisement, and was sorely offended by its example of conspicuous bad grammar from a quasi-official body that should have known better, and was in business to preserve standards, not flout them. Farther down, the advertisement printed Citizens Advice Bureau *sic*, without a possessive apostrophe after Citizens'. The National Association of Citizens Advice Bureaux recently decided to drop its apostrophe, so confounding its genitive, as a matter of policy. Twenty-nine other purists felt strongly enough to write to the Advertising Standards Authority to complain about it.

The Authority considered the complaints for six weeks, and delivered a robust and stylish reply. Its chairman, Lord Thomson of Monifieth, wrote to *The Times* saying that it had been decided as a matter of policy to use colloquial English in the advertisements: 'It was decided *that* in view of the popular character of the advertisement, involving such folk heroes as Marjorie Proops and Sir Matt Busby, *that* the colloquial idiom should be used, rather

166

than the more grammatically exact one.' Either by printer's error, or as a conscious decision to reflect the popular character of *The Times*, the key sentence of his letter contained an error of syntax, by using two *thats* where one would have been sufficient. Lord Thomson wrote defiantly but with good humour to the chief sub-editor of *The Times*, echoing Churchill, that 'your complaint is one up with which we cannot put'.

The case-forms of English have been dying for a thousand years, and those of our pronouns are the last to go. Our grammar is what we decide to make it. Most of us can deal competently with case-forms, even some archaic ones, as when we distinguish between *thou* and *thee* in prayer, without needing to think about it. If we had remained intransigent, conforming to the rules of grammarians who supposed English to be an ossified language like Latin, we should still be saying *ho* instead of *she* and *unc* instead of *us* (two). And when the time for change comes, who decides? Us, of course, as we shall soon be saying. In a century or two *whom* will seem as archaic as *stanum*, the Old English dative plural of *stan*, a stone. But while the cases of pronouns live, they provide useful and elegant distinctions. No doubt the Advertising Standards Authority was aiming at the matey language of the common man, but it could have achieved that without solecism. A body whose name formally states its concern for standards should not join in debasing the standards of English. Or, as the epitaph on the tombstone of a young girl put it:

> 'Her as was has gone from we,
> Us as is will go to she.'

As a red herring or footnote to this, there is a pretty little mystery to the famous Churchill quotation that was used in the argument. According to Sir Ernest Gowers in *Plain Words* Churchill wrote, 'This is the sort of English up with which I will not put,' as a marginal comment on a pedantic piece of officialese, to illustrate the absurd result of strictly applying a grammatical rule. Was Churchill aware that *up*, transposed from the end of the phrase, was an adverb, or did he mistake it for a preposition (which, of course, it can be in other contexts)? How many people who still quote the phrase realize that either it was a bit of mischief by Churchill, or he fell into a trap in his desire to pillory the pedants? Even the most fastidious and crusty grammarian could do no more to the phrase than change 'which I will not put up with' to 'with which I will not put up'.

INDEX

174